# MILLER'S

# MOVIE
## COLLECTIBLES

# Miller's Movie Collectibles
## Rudy & Barbara Franchi

First published in Great Britain in 2002 by Miller's, a division of Mitchell Beazley,
imprints of Octopus Publishing Group Ltd, 2–4 Heron Quays, London E14 4JP

Miller's is a registered trademark of Octopus Publishing Group Ltd

COMMISSIONING EDITOR: Anna Sanderson
EXECUTIVE ART EDITOR: Rhonda Fisher
PROJECT EDITOR: Emily Anderson
DESIGN: Jester Designs
EDITOR: Catherine Blake
PROOFREADER: Miranda Stonor
INDEXER: Sue Farr
PICTURE RESEARCH: Giulia Hetherington
PRODUCTION: Angela Couchman
SPECIAL PHOTOGRAPHY: Steve Tanner

ISBN 1 84000 510 6
A CIP catalogue record for this book is available from the British Library
Set in Gill Sans, Gill Sans Light & Gill Sans Book
PRODUCED BY TOPPAN PRINTING CO., (HK) LTD
PRINTED AND BOUND IN CHINA

Half-title page: *Lawrence of Arabia* 1962 Roadshow six-sheet ($5,000–6,000/£3,325–4,000)
Imprint page: *Dial M for Murder* 1954 UK quad ($3,000–4,000/£2,000–2,675)
Title page: *Hell's Angels* 1930 window card ($2,000–3,000/£1,325–2,000)

# MILLER'S

# MOVIE
## COLLECTIBLES

RUDY & BARBARA FRANCHI

# Contents

Introduction

Volumes have been written about the compulsion to collect but, rising above all the theorizing and psychobabble about why we accumulate objects, one nearly solid fact emerges: what allows us to collect is the new leisure time granted to us by advances in technology. The great 18th- and 19th-century collections that formed the basic holdings of many of the world's major museums were put together by royalty and the upper classes. Stamps, coins, cigarette cards, and postcards were minor hobbies among the masses, but it is really only since the middle of the 20th century that the expanding middle class has been able to turn its attention from endless work to indulge in the passion, seemingly buried deep in human nature, to collect on a massive scale. For example, letters from famous people have long been coveted items, but it is only recently that there has sprung up an entire mini-industry devoted to actually soliciting, and trading in, autographs.

While those with wealth continue to buy major works of art, including contemporary pieces, the new breed of collector focuses on what might well be called pop-culture cast-offs – such ephemera as movie posters, promotional items turned out by the studios, actual props and costumes from films, and all the products and souvenirs bearing the image of favorite movie stars. Collectors fascinated with Hollywood memorabilia have become moths to the flame of cinema's luminaries. What started back in the silent era as a minor hobby, and developed into a raging fad fanned by the studio publicity departments during the early talkie era, has now spawned a thriving business, with major auctions and huge Internet sites devoted to buying, selling, and swapping all the gossip and gimmicks generated by the entertainment industry.

This book outlines some of the major areas of movie memorabilia, highlighting trends and warning of any potential land mines buried deep in the field of cinema collectibles. With over 65 years' combined experience dealing with the topics discussed, the authors would advise collectors to regard acquiring this material as a hobby, and to temper their passion with common sense and caution. Do not be discouraged by early errors – rather view them as tuition in the learning process, as paying one's dues and acquiring a few battle scars are all part of the collecting game. This is doubly true for neophyte dealers. There are no professionals in this field who don't have, buried deep in their inventory, disastrous mistaken purchases made early in their careers. One can read endlessly about movie posters, but nothing educates more quickly than laying out good money only to find you've bought a reproduction. It is certainly an event unlikely to be repeated.

There a few points to make about the guideline prices in the book: many represent recent results at auctions, either live or on the

Internet, or combined averages of several different sales. It is important to note that each guide price is for that specific item only. With movie posters, for example, there are wide variations within the same title depending on size, format, and whether it is an advance or a style variation. For example, the 1942 six-sheet of *Casablanca* illustrated above is the rarest style on the title, with only three known to exist.

A number of publications cite values for several different examples from the same film (*see* the bibliography on p.138). This caveat is also important with autographs: a plain signature by the singer and actress Judy Garland might be valuable, but a handwritten letter by her describing a day's shooting on the set of *The Wizard of Oz* would push that price into the stratosphere.

It would seem that, despite the gentle advice, it all eventually comes down to money, and perhaps that is what collecting has really become – a form of commercial interaction. If that is the case then so be it, but this book can still be used as it was intended – an attempt to share some of the knowledge acquired over many years in the business of movie collectibles, combined with a look at the direction in which prices and values are heading in today's market.

# Posters

Ever since the first moving images appeared on a Paris screen over 100 years ago there have been collectors of film paper, from lowly handbills to huge billboards. As more and more films were produced collectors began to specialize, choosing favorite stars, or posters from specific genres such as westerns, science fiction, or film noir. Two events marked the evolution of a minor hobby into a dealer-driven business: in 1991 a King Kong (1933) poster sold at Christie's, New York, for an unheard-of price of $51,200 (£34,150); in March 1997 The Mummy (1932) poster fetched $453,500 (£302,350) at Sotheby's Manhattan salesrooms – the highest price paid for a movie poster and a record that still stands. These are heady prices for film posters as the vast majority sell for under $1,000 (£650), but since the early 1980s, when even a few hundred dollars was considered a very high price for a used theater advertisement, there has been a huge expansion in the collecting of movie ephemera.

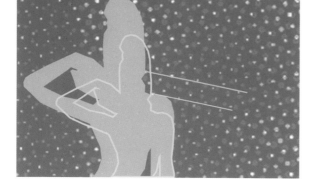

# Poster Sizes

Some hobbies are collector driven and some are dealer driven, and movie posters are definitely the latter. One of the advantages held by dealers is the arcane jargon used to designate various sizes and formats of film paper. The following pages are an attempt to translate the more important terms into plain English. The history of movie-poster collecting is not only a history of film, but a history of paper and printing. Oceans of movie advertising were created during the 20th century and, while only a small fraction survived, it is still a large enough amount to support an active collecting community, controlled by a number of informed aficionados. While this section gives the basic information on sizes, there will be additional comments throughout the book when an interesting variation is presented. This aspect of poster collecting is much like studying a dead language, since almost all the formats discussed are obsolete. But they represent a rich history of promotion and exploitation, which helped build an industry founded on a fragile marriage of greed and dreams and has inspired a whole new generation of fans, not of the movies themselves, but of the myths that they have created.

☆ $4,000–6,000
☆ £2,700–4,000

▲ This classic 1961 poster is a prime example of a U.S. one-sheet, which measured 27 x 41 in, until the mid-'90s when an inch was trimmed from the height to create the current standard of 27 x 40 in (often with ½ in variations.) Like all size designations, "one-sheet" is printing terminology, in this case based on half the size of the printing bed on a late 19th-century stone lithography press. The one-sheet is the basic unit of movie-poster collecting and the value of all sizes is relative to it (e.g. a title lobby card is worth 25%.)

☆ $2,000–3,000
☆ £1,300–2,000

◀ This 1951 three-sheet measures 41 x 81 in, the standard for this format. Most three-sheets come in two sections, as does this one, but in the 1970s a handful of international versions (including *Alien* and *The Godfather*) were made as a single sheet. There are also examples of three sections, mostly from the '30s and '40s. Three-sheets first appeared about 1912 but the size is now obsolete, and has been since the mid-1980s. Often the top or bottom half can be found among old movie posters, but several attempts to create a central system for marrying orphan sections have failed.

◀ The 81 × 81 in six-sheet invariably comes in four sections and this 1961 example captures the power and freedom of design created by the huge square format. The six-sheet was mostly for use outside the theater, and for posting on hoardings around town. While a typical pre-1990 run of one-sheets would be 15,000 to 20,000 posters, only a few thousand three-sheets would be produced for a film, and less than 1,000 six-sheets. This was a difficult size for dealers to sell until the recent boom in loft conversions and the building of enormous mansions gave people the space to display them.

☆ $1,200–1,500
☆ £800–1,000

▼ The 30 × 40 is the smaller brother of the 40 × 60 (see below right) and shares all its attributes except, as with this 1969 example, it is invariably a duplicate image of the one-sheet. It is also one of the few formats that was always sent to movie theaters rolled. Movie paper was traditionally folded at the printing plant so it could travel from theater to theater between the film cans. But in the late 1980s cinemas began to show the films simultaneously, rather than in a cycle, and all posters were sent rolled in tubes.

☆ $2,000–2,500
☆ £1,300–1,700

☆ $300–500
☆ £200–350

▲ Introduced in the early 1930s, the 40 × 60 was silk-screened on light card stock, although, post-1960s, lithography took the place of silk-screening. Sent to movie theaters rolled, they were usually posted on a easel outside the entrance. This *Some Like It Hot* example dates from 1959. Very few of this format were produced – less than 800 per film – and even fewer have survived, hence the relatively high guide price. Often an entirely new image was created for this format and the paper stock and printing method created a dramatic and forceful presentation. In the 1960s and '70s the 40 × 60 poster proved popular for advertising at drive-in movies because of its high visibility and durability.

☆ $1,000–1,200
☆ £650–800

◀ This 1947 half-sheet, measuring 28 × 22 in, demonstrates the design strength of this once-popular size. The landscape format, similar to that of the British quad (see p.14), lends itself to a dramatic graphic presentation that echoes the cinematic aspects of a real movie screen. Often called a "lobby display", it was printed on light card stock until, close to its demise in the 1980s, the later examples appeared on regular poster paper. The image is often identical to the title card in the lobby card set. It came from the printer rolled, but was often folded in half or in quarters for easier transport.

☆ $300–400
☆ £200–270

◀ This 1955 insert derived its name from the instruction that accompanied it – "insert into top of frame." Measuring 14 × 36 in, not all insert images were as powerful as this 1956 Saul Bass creation, but it is a popular format with collectors since it can fill spaces between larger posters and fit into odd corners of a room. Often the image was a pastiche of several campaign design elements. Meant to be rolled, many inserts were folded in thirds for shipping, or for storage by small local theaters who held posters and other promo material in case films returned by popular demand; extra folds were often added to fit the inserts into filing cabinets.

☆ $400–500
☆ £270–330

▲ This 1933 window card, measuring 14 × 22 in, is complete with its blank space at the top, used to announce the location and dates of a film's run. The card was tacked to telephone booths or store windows and the information would be scrawled by hand or printed locally. The window card is one of the few pieces of promo material that was not meant to be returned and the top section was often trimmed for re-use, or by early collectors unaware that it reduced the card's value. Two spin-offs – the jumbo window card (22 × 28 in) and the mini (8 × 14 in) – usually had different art from the regular card but both were rare, and now obsolete.

► Lobby cards are almost always produced in sets of eight, and in many cases the first card is a mini-poster image, as with this example from Capra's 1946 masterpiece. Called the title card, it is often the most valuable in the set. Not all studios created title cards (Paramount omitted them in the 1930s, and Disney in the 1950s), and it is invariably the one card missing when a set is discovered in an old theater or poster exchange. Usually landscape in format, the title card design draws from key elements of the campaign, tempting collectors by the intensity of its image and convenient size.

☆ $800–1,000
☆ £530–670

☆ $500–700
☆ £330–470

▼ Known as front-of-house sets, these 10 x 8 in prints echo the early days of lobby cards, when some were produced in this format. They are usually duplicate images of the U.S. lobby set, with an additional scene card to substitute for the title card. While the term is British, these sets, as with the example shown from *How the West Was Won* (1962), were used in U.S. movie houses too. Usually produced in sets of eight there are variations – Disney produced many sets with nine cards. Often confused with photographic stills, these printed lithographs are seldom produced for films today.

☆ $75–80
☆ £50–55

▲ Between 1908, when lobby-card sets were introduced, and about 1930 there were a few exceptions to eight-card sets (such as larger sets of up to 16, and sets with two title cards) but, as with this 1962 epic, the vast majority comprised seven scene cards and one title card. Advertising coming attractions, they were displayed in the theater lobby, usually in a special wall display area that held eight 14 x 11 in frames. There are some valuable individual cards, especially those that capture a film's mood (the "mad scientist" scene from *Metropolis* (1926) sold for $9,500), and other "dead cards" that portray very little. Lobby-card sets are obsolete in the U.S.A. but still used in Europe and Asia.

☆ $200–300
☆ £130–200

◀ Though one of the scarcest types of movie display material, the jumbo lobby card, measuring 14 × 17 in and produced in limited quantities from the 1920s through the 1940s, is an ideal candidate for aggressive collecting. This 1932 example is in portrait format, but there are also landscape visuals in the set of eight cards. Printed on linen stock, there are no title cards in jumbo sets and the images, which are mostly full bleed with no margin, are completely different from the lobby set. Extra time and effort went into producing these powerful examples of the naive design forces that give early movie advertising its charm and allure, and some sets have sold into the low thousands at auction.

☆ $800–1,000
☆ £530–670

☆ $1,200–1,400
☆ £800–950

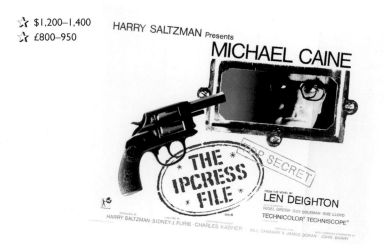

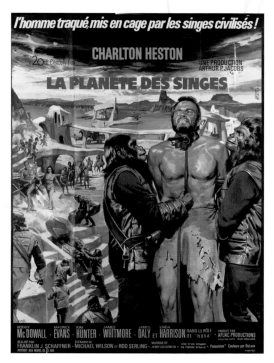

▲ Measuring 40 × 30 in, the British quad is the standard for movie display in the U.K., where all poster sizes are derived from traditional Imperial paper measures. There is a wide range of sizes, most of them infrequently used. This 1965 Michael Caine thriller has a typical quad, in a landscape format with display elements from the campaign key art. The other basic British size is the double crown (20 × 30 in), which is invariably portrait and was used mainly for wall posting and bus advertising. The quad often just rotates the U.S. one-sheet art to fit its horizontal presentation, but there are examples, using completely different artwork and styles, that have become major collectibles, and some attractive and powerful images are generated for films produced in Britain.

▲ The dimensions of the French *grande* (47 × 63 in) were dictated by the size of the European 19th-century lithography presses, used to create the first true posters by masters such as Toulouse-Lautrec. Until recently French posters presented an entirely new treatment of a U.S. title, as with this 1968 example. They were invariably folded and printed on fairly heavy paper stock. There are no dates so it is difficult to detect re-releases, though later ones use mostly thinner, glossier stock. It is best to buy these titles, and most foreign posters, from dealers in the country of origin or U.S. dealers with large stocks of offshore titles.

☆ $600–800
☆ £400–530

Godard's *Le Mépris* was given the English title *Contempt*, which is close to what most collectors and dealers feel for the inconsistency of the smaller French sizes. All posters smaller than a *grande* are called *affichette*, but there are at least three sizes. The classic dimensions are 24 × 32 in, as with the 1962 example left, known as a *moyenne*, but there are other formats, 16 × 24 in and 17 × 25 in (called a *petite*) being the most common. The graphics tend to duplicate those on the *grande*. French posters usually have a censor's number (*visa de censure*), but if there is a second number it indicates the poster is a commercial re-issue.

☆ $1,200–1,500
☆ £800–1,000

The standard Italian size is the *due*, or *2 foglio*, measuring 39 × 55 in and almost always folded and printed on a wide variety of lower-grade paper. Italian artwork and printing often produce the most dramatic international imagery on a title, but the Italians also have the most confusing method of dating posters. The key year to remember is 1966: before then a poster may not have a date (as with the 1954 example right), but after that almost all were printed with either "Primi Edizioni" or "Anno Eddizioni" along the right side. If a poster for a pre-1966 film has these words on it, it is a re-release.

☆ $4,000–5,000
☆ £2,700–3,300

This immense Italian format, 55 × 79 in, is known variously as a *quattro* or *4 foglio* and is usually printed in two sections. As with this poster for *Affair in Trinidad* (1952) with art by Anselmo Ballester, the size brings out the best in Italian poster artists, but most collectors shy away from them because of the unwieldy dimensions. There are several other formats of interest, including the *locandino* (13 × 28 in, with slight variations), which is a cross between a U.S. window card, as it has a blank space for information, and a U.S. insert. *Photobustas*, Italian lobby sets, are printed on glossy, often flimsy paper and come in sets of five and up. They are often sold as individual "posters", and on rare Italian titles can be the only existing printed matter.

◀ A pair of three-sheets from RKO's 1932 king of the monsters illustrates the style variations in posters from the same year of release. For a variety of reasons – to appeal to different audiences, to vary a campaign, or to mask the true nature of a film – studios would issue a style A, B, and even C poster. This was also done to refresh a campaign when a film had been in release for a long period (see the style D *Star Wars* poster on p.87). The examples illustrated have subtle but interesting variations. The style A, far left, shows the classic image of Kong on the Empire State Building – the main key art for the entire campaign. Style B, left, attempts to lure a completely different, and younger, audience by using imagery common to the pulp adventure magazines of the early 1930s, a genre that had captured the imagination, and small change, of teenagers.

▼ Banners, ranging in size from 6 x 4 ft to 12 x 8 ft, were introduced in the 1930s. Like this 1941 example, early banners were silk-screened on canvas and produced in very limited numbers. During the late '40s, and into the '50s, they were printed on heavy paper and had little or no illustrative art. Over the last ten years banners have had a renaissance and are now printed on vinyl in horizontal and vertical formats. Often a series of banners is created for a new release, and up to six unique images decorate the cavernous glass-enclosed "lobbies" of the modern megaplex.

⭐ $400–600
⭐ £270–400

⭐ $80–100
⭐ £55–70

▶ This 1998 poster is a true advance as the artwork by Robert Silver, whose innovative mini-photomontage technique became a shortlived rage, is completely different from the regular-release one-sheet. The advance is placed in theaters weeks, sometimes months, before the film opens. Designers have more freedom since they are not bound by the contractual restrictions of displaying the stars' names, or including the full credits. Fewer advances are printed, so those with different artwork are often worth more than the one-sheet. However, most recent advances are simply the regular poster with an opening date added, and thus differ little in price.

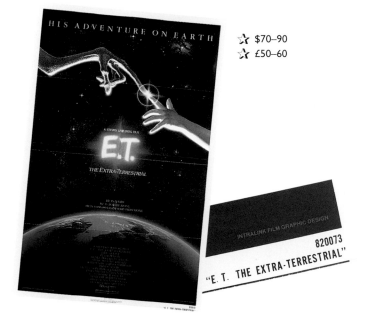

⭐ $70–90
⭐ £50–60

▲ This 1954 French door panel is known as a *pantalon* and measures 23 × 78 in; in the U.S. they are 20 × 60 in, with some larger special editions. Since they often have radically different artwork they are quite sought after. The U.S. panels came in sets, usually of four. The rarest door panels, fetching thousands of dollars at recent auctions, are those from James Bond films, especially the set for *Casino Royale*. Another interesting size is the mini-poster, about 17 × 24 in, given out during the first few days of a film's run.

▲ The numbers in the bottom right corner of most U.S. posters are the National Screen Service code. The first two numbers are the date of the poster (1982) and the rest are stock identification used on all advertising material related to that film. By the end of the 1930s all the major studios were part of the NSS, though some dropped out for brief periods so not all posters carry the code. The prefix R indicates a re-release, and a rubber-stamped date means the original poster was used again for a re-release. If a film is brought back after a few years a new NSS number is assigned; text such as "Back Again", or inferior duo-tone printing, suggests a re-issue.

★ $400–600
★ £275–400

# Silent Films

There is no greater example of the generational nature of movie poster collecting than the gradual but steady decline in value of silent movie material. When the boom in cinema-paper collecting began about 15 years ago, prices for silent-movie lobby cards and one-sheets climbed to dizzying heights, but over the last two or three years only the prime pieces have sold at auction, and there are just a few dealers around today who make a market in pre-talkie items. The older collectors who bid up silent memorabilia are fading away, as are those who once overpaid for mundane 1930s inserts and window cards. Now the demand is for '50s science fiction, '60s neo-noir and '70s spaghetti westerns. The mega-collectors and a handful of deep-pocketed institutions will always pick up a *Metropolis* three-sheet, a *Jazz Singer* half-sheet, or great Keaton, Lloyd, or Chaplin ephemera, but the oceans of silent film material on the market are choked with floating mines, and care should be taken when buying what appears to be a bargain.

▲ Buster Keaton is the very essence of what silent movies were all about. His inventiveness in creating first-time special effects was reflected in his ability to make one feel that the unreal could really happen. *The General*, released in 1926, was Keaton at his best. Illustrator Hap Hadley did the entire campaign, and the border design on this lobby card is derived from his key art (the campaign's main image). The title card can sell for as high as $2,500 (£1,675), and one picturing the train from the film can fetch around $1,500 (£1,000).

★ $10–15
★ £7–10

▲ This 1922 lobby card, in poor condition, from a non-descript film starring Pauline Frederick, is included here as a typcial example of early to mid-'20s material for sale in today's movie marketplace. There may be a handful of Pauline Frederick collectors out there, but they cannot drive a market when there is so much material available. Don't be tempted into thinking it must surely sell at a higher price one day. It takes both scarcity and rarity to force up prices and maintain a value base.

◄ The value of this little-known film, *Harp Of Tara*, lies in its extremely early date (1914, just two years after the first ever feature, *The Birth Of A Nation*) and the process by which it was printed. Most posters of the silent era were stone lithos, created using crayon on Bavarian limestone (for which each color required an individual pass over the press). Even after the introduction of metal plates to the lithography process, posters were called stone lithos to distinguish this entire process from the offset printing methods that predominated from the 1930s.

▼ The major printers of the silent era, such as Morgan Litho and J.H. Tooker, produced a vast amount of posters (finding mention of a printer on a poster is a strong indication of an original release), but this stone litho from 1915 has all the attributes of quality printing that collectors seek. Stone lithography can be distinguished from offset printing by close examination with a magnifying glass. The dots on a stone litho are random, but quite regular on an offset print. Stone lithos seem to glow, and when one sees just a few the differences become obvious. They are stellar examples of the printer's craft.

▲ Gloria Swanson's career spanned over 60 years, but it was *Sunset Boulevard* (1950), about a silent-film star, that lodges in the memory, along with Norma Desmond's famous line "we had faces then." This 1937 window card shows what she meant, as the artists who created the image were well aware of the power of Swanson's visage. The space found at the top of most window cards has here been filled in with printed information, rather than with the usual crayoned scrawl. This particular card has been auctioned three times for roughly the same price. Some movie papers float from sale to sale in a collector/dealer diaspora, briefly loved and then found boring.

▲ The value of this title card for *Grandma's Boy* (1922) lies not only in its association with Harold Lloyd but also in the fact that it is an important indicator of Hollywood's growing reliance on the "star" system. Rather than portray a scene from the film, the card merely features Lloyd in his signature spectacles. Images of stars became a semiotic shorthand for the type of movie they appeared in. It is interesting that in these early days of cinema, the director and star were often the same person – a continuation of the great actor/manager tradition of the U.S. and British stage that was submerged by the '30s and the rise of the studio system, only to surface again in the '60s.

▲ This beautifully designed and executed 1917 one-sheet marks the poster's transition from the promotion of Wild West shows to movies. This is a fitting example, as it was Buffalo Bill Cody who perfected the use of the poster to publicize his spectacular "shoot 'em up" extravaganzas, relying on billboard advertising as his main method of attracting crowds. He used a huge variety, in sizes never seen again: 24- or 32-sheet layouts and, in 1898, a record-breaking 168-sheet poster that wrapped around an entire building.

▶ Rudolph Valentino was cinema's first great male star, and his appearance in 1921's *The Four Horsemen of the Apocalypse* propelled him to an unprecedented height of public recognition that is hard to appreciate today. In the '20s it was one star at a time, and Valentino dominated the screen and media. His death was a national event, causing several fans to commit suicide. A vast amount of Valentino-related material was generated, but such is the continuing hunger among collectors that there is a constant paucity of it on the market. Posters for his films are very scarce and even period stills, often the most attainable of collectibles, are hard to come by.

▶ This 1917 stone litho for *The Other Man* bears four names of importance: Roscoe (Fatty) Arbuckle, whose career was nearing its peak (only to be extinguished by a famous murder trial in 1921); Mack Sennett, the acknowledged King of Comedy, who discovered a host of stars during the 1910s and '20s, including Chaplin; and the production companies, Keystone and Triangle, which, along with other names such as Mutual and First National, melted away with the advent of sound and the rise of the majors. A few companies like Warner, MGM, and Twentieth Century-Fox survived. Now well aware of the value of a brand name, they spend huge sums promoting not only the films but also the studio itself.

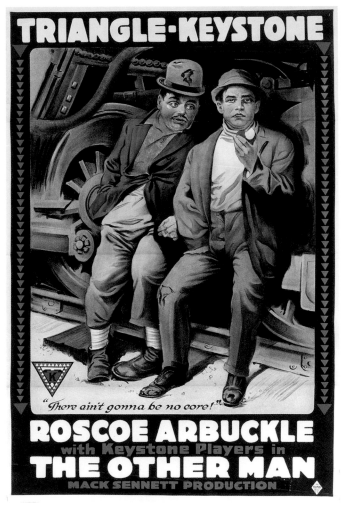

◀ This 1926 one-sheet advertising a magazine promoting movie-going is interesting for its early mention of the "Motion Picture Theatre Owners of America" – a group that was to become quite powerful. While the major studios owned a vast number of movie theaters (until 1948 when they were declared a monopoly and forced to divest), in smaller cities and towns there were still thousands of privately owned neighborhood movie houses (or "nabes," as *Variety* called them) which were the backbone of the industry. A small but distinct group of collectors exists for material concerned with the actual functioning of the business, and prices are often quite reasonable.

# KEYSTONE COMEDY TO·DAY

⭐ $300–400
⭐ £200–275

◀ Here is a glorious example of a promotional poster for Mack Sennett's production company. Along with the number of stars he discovered, his greatest creation was the Keystone Kops – a phrase that has entered the language and a style of comedic action that lives to this day. Dating from about 1919, this one-sheet is associated with one of the key figures of the silent era, and is masterfully printed, yet its price languishes in the low hundreds – proof that it is the stars of particular movies, rather than the producers, that create a demand for collectibles.

⭐ $5,000–6,000
⭐ £3,325–4,000

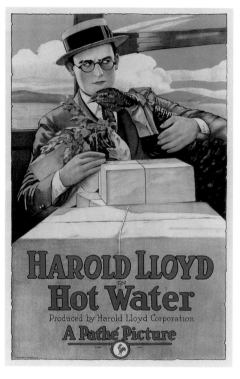

⭐ $7,000–8,000
⭐ £4,675–5,325

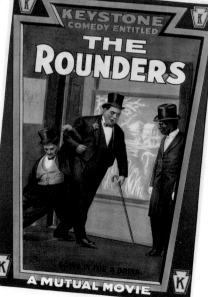

▶ Firsts are always important in collecting and this 1914 one-sheet is the earliest Chaplin poster yet discovered. He is shown dragged along by Fatty Arbuckle, both uncredited and both just starting careers that would be marred by scandal. The price range for this poster is a comment on collecting trends: it sold for this amount the one time it appeared on the market, at an auction in New York in 2000. A few years earlier it might well have made five times that sum, but in the intervening years several major Chaplin collectors turned their attention to other types of film posters. It doesn't take much to deflate a market maintained by just a handful of deep pockets.

▲ When *Hot Water* was released in 1924 Harold Lloyd was at the peak of his career. No other example of this amazing poster exists. It is a masterpiece of design, the perspective of the stacked packages creating an almost three-dimensional effect. The image of Lloyd clutching a turkey set against a cloud-filled sky borders on the surreal, capturing the tone of what was rather a bizarre movie. While such rarefied examples of poster art are hard to come by on the marketplace, collectors should not lose heart. This one was found behind a wall during the renovation of a derelict Canadian cinema, and the proceeds from its sale were put towards its reopening.

☆ $700–900
☆ £475–600

◀ Certain posters seem to have a career in the marketplace and this 1923 one-sheet fits that description. Over the years different examples have shown up at auction and one begins to suspect that someone has discovered a small quantity of them, had them all linen-mounted and restored, and has assiduously been placing them for sale over a well-spaced period. It is interesting that it maintains its price level, almost always selling in the same range. It has shown up in newly opened restaurants and its food theme makes it an ideal decoration for kitchen/dining areas. Jackie Coogan was the first great child star, and gave his name to a California law that protects the earnings and assets of young entertainers after his parents invested and lost his fortune in a series of harebrained schemes.

☆ $30,000–35,000
☆ £20,000–23,300

▶ The Jazz Singer is included here not in its capacity as the first sound film but rather as the last silent film. Released in 1927 it revolutionized the industry, but apart from the musical numbers there were actually only a few words of spoken dialogue. After this, almost everything else in the distribution pipeline quickly had a soundtrack added. This half-sheet is the only one ever discovered in this format and is a rare example of the black face campaign that had been created for the film as a B style. (The key art is the famous scene of Jolson sitting at the piano with his mother.) Once more, take heart – this poster was discovered in a Boston coal cellar, sandwiched between two damaged half-sheets.

# Serials, Series, and Stock Posters

Relating stories in weekly chapters has a pedigree far removed from Saturday afternoon two-reelers. Many of the great 19th-century novels, by such masters as Charles Dickens, were presented in installments over a period of time. The movie serial was born in France, early in cinema history with the 1908 Nick Carter series, which simply broke up a film into sections. The first true serial, with each part ending with a teasing cliffhanger, was *What Happened to Mary*, which appeared in 1913. Its 13 chapters, each lasting 20 minutes, became the standard for over 40 years, until the very last serial, *Blazing the Overland Trail* (1956), marked the end of the tradition – killed no doubt by the episodic nature of TV programming. The serial evolved into the movie series – each film complete in itself but having a common set of characters as, for example, in the *Charlie Chan* films. Thousands of films were produced in series form, and most appeared in the cinema as the second half of a double bill. Collecting serial paper in particular is a passion fraught with pitfalls, since the same serials were released repeatedly, and very few of the posters or lobby cards indicate this.

▲ Every studio had a B picture unit that turned out series with an assortment of characters and themes. One of the most famous series was *Sherlock Holmes* – a dozen-plus movies made in the early 1940s, starring Basil Rathbone and Nigel Bruce. The movie paper is subject to severe cross-pressure from film collectors and fans of Holmes. The three-sheet and one-sheet from *Pursuit To Algiers* (1945) and the one-sheet from *Terror By Night* (1946) illustrate the graphic similarity of series posters. As with the films themselves, the promotional concept was to make them easily identifiable and consistent in mood.

The studios issued copious movie paper to promote their serials, but mostly not of the same printing quality as the regular releases. There was usually a master one-sheet, displayed for the entire cycle of chapters. Often this would be a stock poster, with a blank space for the chapter title to be written in each week. Many serials had four lobby cards issued for each chapter; this one is from the 12th chapter of *G-Men vs. The Black Dragon* (1944). Serial paper rarely has NSS numbers or dates, but re-release material is often worn and poorly printed.

☆ $40–50
☆ £25–35

☆ $40–50
☆ £25–35

▲ As with many serial and series characters, Dick Tracy was born in another medium – the famed comic strip created by Chester Gould. His first screen appearances were in four Saturday matinee programs produced by Republic in the late 1930s and early '40s. In 1945 RKO decided to revive the sleuth in a series of four feature films; the lobby card illustrated is from the first of those. With a fairly limited market, values of material from post-war series have remained modest, and major items from the earlier serials trade at best in the low thousands.

▼ Even in the backwater world of serial production there was a pecking order, and the trio of *Flash Gordon* space-opera cliff-hangers were the most famous and best promoted of the genre. This one-sheet is a 1947 re-release from the last serial, first shown in 1940. The use of colour indicates the near feature-film status the films were awarded by Universal. All three serials were recycled into features (a common practice, turning a serial into a series), and the one-sheet for the first film is the most valuable, selling for $40,000–50,000.

☆ $500–600
☆ £325–400

☆ $600–800
☆ £400–525

▲ This French poster, with art by Joseph Koutachy, was issued in the 1940s and illustrates the stock poster format that was used extensively for cartoons, newsreels, and many of the shorts and/or featurettes that cinemas showed between the double features. Any *Three Stooges* paper attracts the most committed and fanatical group of collectors in the movie-ephemera world, with early black-and-white posters, which are one-of-a-kind but have no graphic interest, making $100,000 at auction.

One of the first landmarks of early cinema was a science-fiction film, Georges Méliès' 1902 special-effects masterpiece, *A Trip to the Moon*. Some fundamentalist movie historians feel that the entire cinema art form reached its peak in the early 1930s, as evidenced by the horror classics produced by Universal Studios. While absolutely no paper exists on Méliès' pioneering French film, and prices of posters for the *Frankenstein*, *Dracula*, and *The Mummy* films are out of reach for mere mortals, thousands of other examples do exist, and auctions at the major houses, as well as the constant flow of material across the Internet, assure a supply of quality items. While much material is available, there is a large number of collectors snapping it up, so prices are forever escalating. With recent releases in particular, it often pays to accumulate prime-condition posters as soon as they appear on the market. Horror and science fiction (the border is often blurred) remain the most popular genres among collectors of entertainment memorabilia in general, and of poster art in particular.

☆ $400–500
☆ £275–325

▲ As this 1954 horror classic opened around the world it inspired poster artists in a number of countries to create distinctive versions. Above is the French *petite*; the *grande* also has strikingly different and disturbingly eerie graphics. Foreign paper on *The Creature from the Black Lagoon* is in fact the best way to add to one's collection since the U.S. original one-sheet trades in the $7,000 (£4,675) range and a three-sheet can cost double that. Any lobby card, insert, window card, or half-sheet showing the monster is desirable.

☆ $400–500
☆ £275–325

▲ Despite the paper shortage during World War II much advertising ephemera was produced and still exists on this relatively obscure title, released in 1944 by Republic (one of the small "poverty row" companies). The industry made such a huge effort to help with the sale of war bonds that it was granted all types of exceptions from production restrictions and rationing. This one-sheet creates a striking effect but the relatively low price indicates that collectors look for more than just a pretty picture.

☆ $400–600
☆ £275–400

◀ Collecting Karloff and collecting horror titles is often the same hobby. Cited as the ultimate example of the typecast actor, Karloff played an unending string of monster and mad scientist roles. Occasional escapes into comedies or even dramas demonstrated his superior talents as an actor, but he was dragged back to horror movies again and again, and ended his career parodying his earlier triumphs. *The Ape*, released in 1940, is typical Karloff fare. Usually a script was written around his availability and not too much attention was paid to the finer points of dialogue or plot. The creator of the one-sheet illustrated was obviously influenced by the 1930s photomontage motif pioneered by European poster designers.

☆ $800–1,000
☆ £525–675

☆ $400–500
☆ £275–325

▲ It is difficult to find a modern film whose impact on the industry can compare with the seismic effect *Frankenstein* had when it came out in 1931. The movie created a franchise that produced not only sequels but also entire parallel series, re-makes, comedic take-offs, a TV series, and oft-misquoted phrases that confuse creator with creature. This is the 1951 lobby card, as issued by Universal's re-release arm, Realart, which obviously didn't stint when it came to design and printing quality. Such re-issue material is quite collectible. The original release version sells in the $5,000 (£3,325) range.

▲ Nobody ever calls it *The Thing From Another World*, but that is its full title. Although a chilling piece of graphic design, this one-sheet would have sold for far more if it had portrayed the creature itself, or perhaps its flying saucer. The 1951 film's direction is credited to Christian Nyby, whose career otherwise holds no indication of such genius. Close examination of several scenes bears out the suspicion that Orson Welles, who was on the RKO lot at the time, contributed his considerable talents. The three- and six-sheets repeat the scary-type style motif with the addition of a trail of blood, and the insert and half-sheet sell at a premium because they contain actual scenes from the film.

☆ $80–100
☆ £55–65

◄ ▼ This pair of U.K. double crowns are two of the most powerful images on this masterful 1991 thriller directed by Jonathan Demme. The U.S. campaign shared the same theme, with the be-skulled winged insect, but it used images of both Foster and Hopkins. The poster shown below is the teaser, as it does not state the title of the film, and the blood-red image is an advance, displaying the title but no credits. Every "Great Movie Posters" list appearing recently includes an example from this film. A group of collectors looking for an edge rushed to buy one-sheets for *Manhunter*, based on the novel introducing Hannibal Lecter, but not even fervid speculation could raise the price of an ugly poster above the $80 mark.

☆ $150–200
☆ £100–125

★ $1,000–2,000
★ £675–1,325

▶ *King Kong* firmly established RKO as a major studio and its massive success led to the creation of an entire genre of films featuring creatures driven to violence by confinement. The original 1933-release lobby card (top) is one of the lesser examples. While all the cards show Kong in the border design (using the Style A campaign art), those in which he appears in the main picture sell for at least three times the value of the one showing the "ledge scene."

The window card (right) is from a 1942 re-release, when a whole new sales effort was created, and only two of these have surfaced so far. If one is ever found from the original campaign, it could sell for about $30,000 (£20,000).

★ $3,000–4,000
★ £2,000–2,675

★ $150–200
★ £100–125

◀ A Polish poster for a Japanese monster movie sounds like an unlikely collectible, until one examines the image. This is the Zbobrowski art for the '80s Polish release of the 1971 film *Godzilla vs. The Smog Monster*, and it is a fine example of the visually intriguing graphics produced in that country from the post-war era up to the end of the Cold War. In the early '90s Polish posters deteriorated into mere copies of the U.S. campaigns, replacing the old artistically personal and often bizarre interpretations. Recently things have improved, but it's doubtful that there will ever be a return to that golden age when the title of the film was often a mystery, but the design of the poster was a joy to behold.

**Julie Christie · Oskar Werner**

DANS UN FILM DE
**François Truffaut**

**Fahrenheit 451**

TECHNICOLOR®

UNE PRODUCTION
VINEYARD FILMS Ltd
RELEASED BY UNIVERSAL
International

CYRIL CUSACK · ANTON DIFFRING · JEREMY SPENSER · ALEX SCOTT

François Truffaut et Jean-Louis Richard — Ray Bradbury — François Truffaut — Lewis M. Allen

☆ $600–800
☆ £400–525

◀ It is painful when a bad film is made of a widely admired book, and though François Truffaut is undoubtedly one of the masters of cinema, Ray Bradbury's *Fahrenheit 451* is one project that he should have passed on. Aside from the noted New Wave auteur's inability to speak English, it is rather ironic that the land of Jules Verne and Georges Méliès does not have a great cinematic track record when it comes to science-fiction movies. However, what does work is Guy Gérard Noel's artwork for this 1967 French *grande*. Far superior to the U.S. poster, it does much to capture the novella's chilling indifference to intellectual destruction.

☆ $100–125
☆ £65–85

THE DIRECTOR OF
"BATMAN" & "BEETLEJUICE"
INVITES YOU TO MEET
HIS NEWEST CREATION:

edward
SCISSORHANDS

☆ $30–40
☆ £20–25

*Cat People*

A HORROR FANTASY ABOUT
THE ANIMAL IN US ALL

NASTASSIA KINSKI · MALCOLM McDOWELL · JOHN HEARD · ANNETTE O'TOOLE

▶ This 1982 film was a remake of Jacques Tourneur's 1942 horror classic, and while the one-sheet for that version is considered a great example of the poster as illustration, this chilling photo treatment of Nastassja Kinski typifies a whole new style of graphic design perfected in the early '80s. In some cases artwork was made to look photographic, and in others scenes from the film were manipulated to create images ranging from romantic impressionism to chilling super-reality, reflecting the mood of this re-release version of *Cat People*. Several dealers are holding quantities of the one-sheet on this title (thanks to anomalies in the distribution system), which depresses the price of what should be a more valuable collectible.

▲ This advance one-sheet for the 1990 film *Edward Scissorhands* was designed by Jeffrey Bacon with a photo credited to Zade Rosenthal and, like some of the clever promotional items created for the movie, it perfectly captures its dark comedic mood. The elevated price for what is a fairly recent film poster is another unintended consequence of technology: the movie had modest success but took on a life of its own after its release to video stores. Its enduring shelf-life as a weekend rental has created a horde of collectors who are almost a renewable resource.

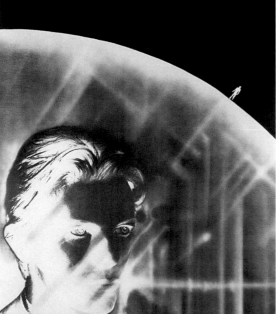

**You have to believe it to see it**

**David Bowie** in
**The man who fell to Earth**

**Cinema I & Cinema II**

◀ Known as the Cinema One Negative Style, this 30 × 45 poster was specially created for a New York movie theater owned by art-movie house pioneer Donald Rugoff. Cinemas One and Two on Third Avenue were the venues for American premieres of many foreign and U.S. independent films that are now considered classics. Often dissatisfied with the mundane artwork created by cash-strapped distributors for the films he showed, Rugoff would commission displays designed to be used just at his movie houses. Most have long since disappeared, but a few posters for *The Man Who Fell to Earth* still circulate in the marketplace.

▶ Based on a featurette he made while still a student, *THX 1138* was expanded to full length by George Lucas and released in 1971. The film was inspired by George Orwell's *1984* and generally greeted by critics with praise for the visuals but disdain for the script. This poster's price may therefore be more a reflection of the director's later fame than of the film itself, or any inherent value it has as a one-sheet. It has fetched some dizzying sums at auction (over $1,100 in one case), but there were too many copies around to keep the price above the range stated here. Always take auction prices with a pinch of salt, as there is no telling what will happen when two people lock themselves into a bidding war.

**The Future is here.**
**THX 1138**

Warner Bros. presents THX 1138 · An American Zoetrope Production · Starring Robert Duvall and Donald Pleasence · with Don Pedro Colley, Maggie McOmie and Ian Wolfe · Technicolor® · Techniscope® · Executive Producer, Francis Ford Coppola · Screenplay by George Lucas and Walter Murch · Story by George Lucas Produced by Lawrence Sturhahn · Directed by George Lucas · Music by Lalo Schifrin

◁ *The Adventures of Buckaroo Banzai Across The 8th Dimension*, to give this 1984 film its full title, is the classic example of a cult film that exists because of its appeal as an entry-level collectible. Not too long ago it would have come and gone through the movie distribution system, leaving a minor ripple and inspiring a handful of devotees to seek out advertising items to remember it by. Cable TV, the VCR, and DVD players not only keep films like this alive (a mixed blessing to some), but also constantly introduce it to new audiences who, if taken with it, then drive up the price of what should be a $20 one-sheet to ten times that amount. Enjoyable but often incoherent, this is a good example of a film that young collectors "grow out of," creating a constant flow of recycled collectibles on the title.

▷ Much has been written about 1950s science-fiction films being thinly disguised symbolic portrayals of Cold War fear. Supposedly the monsters, out-of-control robots, and alien invaders were really stand-ins for a shifting cast of enemies. *The Day the Earth Stood Still* might well serve as the ultimate example of this, but to movie-paper collectors it is just a great poster for a favorite film. The image on this original release one-sheet (1951) has been endlessly reproduced, and collectors should be aware that there are precise facsimiles on the market. The usual points of distinction give them away: the paper is too new, the back of the poster is a flat bright white, and the image lacks the crispness of the original. One should attend auction previews and good galleries to a get a feel for what vintage posters look like.

☆ $200–400
☆ £125–275

▶ Awaited with growing dread is the announcement of "Mad Max: The Musical," for this series of Australian science-fiction films has a devoted enough following to ensure a lengthy run. Shown here are the 40 x 60s for the first two films of the trilogy. They command prices about 30% above the one-sheet because of their larger, more dramatic format and unfolded condition. *Mad Max* released in 1979 in the U.S. as an exploitation thriller and American voices were dubbed onto the soundtrack. Not until the huge success of the sequel *Road Warrior* (1981) did the first film find a major audience, and posters and other paper on the original release are quite hard to come by. Daybills are also desirable (see p.36), but Australian dealers and collectors are loathe to see them leave the country.

☆ $600–800
☆ £400–525

☆ $100–200
☆ £65–125

◀ One wonders if Ridley Scott and art director Douglas Trumbull predicted the look of today's Times Square, or if that New York landmark's creators were inspired by the film. Either way, *Blade Runner* has become a design term associated with futuristic, message-cluttered cityscapes. Both science fiction and film noir, this 1982 film, based on a Philip K. Dick novel, has a devoted following and any paper on it is collectible, especially this one-sheet and the U.S. and high-quality German lobby card sets. The poster was designed by John Alvin, who has completed a revised 20th-anniversary version (with Rutger Hauer at upper right.) There is also a 1992 director's cut poster selling for about a quarter of the original. One reproduction makes regular appearances, betrayed by its slight blurriness.

$1,800–2,000
£1,200–1,325

"Open on: night time, a rain-slicked street reflects lamp lights and a flashing neon sign. Cut to: a seedy hotel room and blue wisps of cigarette smoke trapped in light filtered through a Venetian blind." These are classic script directions for a film noir. The term is derived from "*roman noir*," used by French literary critics to describe 19th-century gothic novels. Later Parisian film writers adapted it to denote a group of Hollywood movies of the '40s and '50s, often made by such European émigré directors as Fritz Lang. The films share certain characteristics, mainly portrayals of a gloomy underworld peopled by disillusioned and apathetic anti-heroes. The visual elements of film noir are often just ways of underlighting cheap sets and utilizing other cost-cutting devices, since they were mostly low-budget B movies slated for the bottom half of a double bill. The European, mainly German Expressionist, touch is evident in the bizarre camera angles and the confident ability to do more with less. Once a genre in retrospect, it has now become a self-conscious and often affected style, with most modern examples being sad attempts at doing on purpose what was once so easy to do by accident.

$500–600
£325–400

▲ Even in the crazy world of collectible movie posters there are certain rules, and one is that the half-sheet usually sells for a bit less than the one-sheet. But when it comes to *Murder My Sweet* (1944) there is an even greater disparity, and that is because of the genre. Film noir collectors want their posters to be as dark and moody as their films: the smaller paper makes the film look like a straight gangster movie, while the larger example reflects all the dark undertones that give a morbid charm to the directorial style. The film gave Dick Powell (leading man in second-rate musicals), a new image as a tough guy. Based on Raymond Chandler's *Farewell My Lovely*, it was re-made in 1975 under that title.

◀ Leave it to a European director to create one of the great modern examples of the film noir genre. Roman Polanski's *Chinatown* puts a 1970s spin on noir, and weaves the seedy side of 1930s Los Angeles right into the film's plot, making the storyline as important as any of the characters. The poster art by Jim Pearsall, with its Art Nouveau overtones and vivid color field technique, is considered one of the major modern campaigns. The same imagery is carried throughout the U.S. paper and, for once, the foreign poster designers could find nothing to improve upon, so all the European advertising is consistent in repeating the original motif.

☆ $800–1,000
☆ £525–675

☆ $500–700
☆ £325–475

▼ If this 1946 adaptation of a tawdry 1930s James Cain novel had come any later it might have been considered a parody of the genre instead of the paradigm it has become. The book's major element, a steamy but doomed romance supercharged with blatant eroticism, was toned down for the film, creating a torrid subtext. If the poster art was any darker the two leads would be invisible but, like the film itself, it stops just short of going too far. All of the paper is popular, especially the lobby cards highlighting the more outrageous scenes.

☆ $3,000–4,000
☆ £2,000–2,675

☆ $400–600
☆ £275–400

▲ In his third feature, *The Killing* (1956), ostensibly a clever caper movie built around a complicated racetrack robbery, Stanley Kubrick creates a parallel movie involving the twisted private lives of the participants that could stand alone as a film noir. The one-sheet pictured (above top) is very much of the 1950s garish design school, playing up the violence. It is the half-sheet (above) that exploits these elements to an extreme in one of the most bizarre pieces of poster paper in the history of movie advertising. Recreating the final moment of the pivotal shoot-out after the robbery, the designer has created a haunting and grotesque image of charnel chaos.

THAT "DIRTY DOZEN" MAN IS BACK!

Metro-Goldwyn-Mayer presents
A Judd Bernard-Irwin Winkler Production

LEE MARVIN
"POINT BLANK"

There are two kinds of people in his up-tight world:
his victims and his women. And sometimes you can't tell them apart.

co-starring
ANGIE DICKINSON
KEENAN WYNN · CARROLL O'CONNOR · LLOYD BOCHNER · MICHAEL STRONG
Screenplay by Alexander Jacobs and David Newhouse & Rafe Newhouse
Directed by John Boorman Produced by Judd Bernard and Robert Chartoff
In Panavision®and Metrocolor MGM

⭐ $600–800
⭐ £400–525

⭐ $40–60
⭐ £25–40

LEE MARVIN
LE POINT DE NON RETOUR

ANGIE DICKINSON
KEENAN WYNN · CARROLL O'CONNOR · LLOYD BOCHNER · MICHAEL STRONG

HET DODE PUNT

There are
two kinds
of people in his
up-tight world:
his victims
and his women.
And sometimes
you can't tell
them apart.

Metro-Goldwyn-Mayer presents
A Judd Bernard-Irwin Winkler
Production

SUITABLE
ONLY FOR
ADULTS

LEE MARVIN
"POINT BLANK"

ANGIE DICKINSON    KEENAN WYNN
CARROLL O'CONNOR · LLOYD BOCHNER · MICHAEL STRONG
Screenplay by Alexander Jacobs and David Newhouse & Rafe Newhouse
Directed by John Boorman Produced by Judd Bernard and Robert Chartoff
In Panavision® and Metrocolor MGM

◀ ▲ Ignored when it was first released in 1967, *Point Blank* is now considered a major work of noir revival. The three posters illustrated carry a range of messages about movie-paper collecting. The U.S. three-sheet (far left), displaying the standard key art by Serrano, sells for a little more than the one-sheet. The center poster is the Australian daybill, similar in size to the U.S. insert but printed on much thinner paper stock. Just as thin is the market for them; Americans don't know this format, and although there are some desirable examples they should be purchased only from reputable dealers. The same can be said for Belgian posters like the one shown above.

⭐ $60–80
⭐ £40–55

⭐ $200–250
⭐ £125–175

▶ If Pacino's performance in this 1975 film was over the top it was matched by the enthusiasm of the Warner Brothers promotion department. They produced four distinct posters for this bizarre movie, about a bank robbery that was really a cry for attention. While Pacino chewed the scenery a team of uncredited illustrators created some very collectible paper, especially the International one-sheet illustrated here. Internationals are posters created for the non-U.S. market and, while often the regular release one-sheet is used without an MPAA rating (the quickest way to identify this category), at times a completely new poster is created. The prominent use of a gun would not work abroad today as several countries have banned all posters with any obvious display of firearms. This has led to the creation of Internationals that delete this imagery from the American-release versions.

In August, 1972, Sonny Wortzik robbed a bank.
250 cops, the F.B.I., 8 hostages and 2,000 onlookers
will never forget what took place.

AL PACINO
DOG DAY
AFTERNOON

▶ As one of the major film noirs, *D.O.A.* (Dead On Arrival) has all the right elements: Director Rudloph Mate had worked as a cameraman in Europe; it was filmed on the streets of L. A. and San Francisco in classic Expressionist style and almost completely at night, and the hero is totally confused as to why he has been given slow-acting poison for which he must find an antidote by dawn. This 1950 lobby card is a favorite with collectors – it is the eighth in the set, and is referred to as the "luminous fluid" image. It captures the mood of the film, and the expression on Edmund O'Brien's face is indicative of the superb acting job he turned in. The one-sheet for this title sells for just over $1,000 (£675).

☆ $200–300
☆ £125–200

☆ $800–900
☆ £525–600

◀ James Cagney was famous for straight-out old-fashioned gangster films, not noir, and *White Heat* certainly seems to be another underworld shoot-'em-up, until actually viewed. Director Raoul Walsh, who earned his noir credentials a decade earlier, is the force that pushes this 1949 movie into the genre category, and he does it by surrounding the violence with mood and delving deeply into the character of the psychopathic hood Cagney so brilliantly portrays. One can also tell this isn't a gangster movie by the price of its paper, which is consistently low across all formats. Meanwhile titles from the 1930s, such as *Public Enemy*, sell at multiples of ten or more above this guide price. This insert for *White Heat* is always popular, combining a strong graphic of the star with a clear, almost lobby-card-like image from the film.

☆ $25–30
☆ £15–20

▶ Raoul Walsh's rather bland directorial style belied his real talent – the ability to tell us what motivated his characters. Bogart's portrayal of the anti-hero gangster in *High Sierra* is one of his best roles, and the depressing atmosphere in the first part of the film sets the tone for the famed end sequence. Illustrated is the 1956 re-release lobby card of this 1941 production. This was the second '50s re-issue (the first was in 1952), marking a time when studios were desperate to win audiences back from TV. It is a classic re-release card, poorly printed in duotones on cheap stock, and worth about a tenth of the original.

☆ $2,500–3,000
☆ £1,675–2,000

◄ When Columbia Pictures president Harry Cohn first saw this film he offered $10,000 to anyone who could explain the plot to him. Someone has yet to collect, as any attempt to make sense of the series of actions in *The Lady From Shanghai* (it's a stretch to call it a plot) is as hard as trying to remember an unusually strange dream. This 1948 film is noir gone bizarre and, like the amusement park sequence at the end, the only thing to do is go along for the ride. The designer who created this one-sheet is unknown but it is one of the masterstrokes of movie poster art. One feels that, for a brief moment, the designer glimpsed the film's true message: Welles' obsession with his wife, Rita Hayworth, and his fear of losing her.

☆ $1,200–1,400
☆ £800–925

☆ $400–500
☆ £275–325

► During the 1950s a Hungarian melody was released in the U.S. as "Gloomy Sunday" and banned from the radio after it was blamed as the cause of several suicides. *It Always Rains on Sunday* could be just as dangerously depressing. More a film *grise* than a film noir, it is relentlessly dreary in its depiction of London's lower depths, but its director, Robert Hamer, created a fascinating film. Illustrated is a U.K. one-sheet – a very rare style that measures 27 x 40 in. This format was not created for every title and there is no pattern as to why or when they were produced: there are major films that have none and many minor films that have both a quad and one-sheet.

▲ This is international noir at its best, and the first of what was to become a distinct sub-genre – the darkly sinister Cold War movie. The film's exterior sequences were shot in post-war Vienna, a perfect setting for this story of black-market double-dealing. The relentless but effective zither score works wonders and helped make the 1949 film a hit, along with Carol Reed's brilliant direction, Graham Greene's original script, and stellar performances by all. It is often cited as "the perfect film." This U.S. one-sheet has no NSS markings or printed information and was probably created to be used in several markets, as the film was independently released by its producer.

The *Blue Dahlia* (1946) is a genre favorite, with an inspired script by Raymond Chandler and Veronica Lake at her deceptively innocent best. Pictured left is the Italian *due*, with art by Regia. When the graphics work in this large format they are overpowering, and this is one of those times when it is worth while giving up a bit of wall space. Below is a style not often seen outside its country of origin, the Australian one-sheet (27 x 40 in). It often features totally different artwork from the U.S. one-sheet, or even from its paper compatriot, the daybill. The red circled warning "Not Suitable For General Exhibition" is a handy dating device as it was dropped in 1971 for letter ratings.

$600–700
£400–475

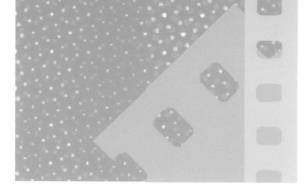

# French, British, and U.S. New Wave

☆ $300–400
☆ £200–275

Buried deep in an article in a French weekly newspaper on the eve of the 1959 Cannes Film Festival was the phrase "nouvelle vague." It was picked up by the American press, with help from the head of publicity for Unifrance Film in New York, and soon stories appeared about a "new wave" of cinema. The Festival saw the triumph of François Truffaut's *Les 400 Coups (The 400 Blows)*, which became the signature film of a movement that was to sweep up every director under the age of 30. At its core were the film critics turned directors from the auteurist publication *Cahiers Du Cinéma*, such as Jean-Luc Godard, Claude Chabrol, and Alain Resnais. It was not long before any French director with a film about to open was included, and then the label spread to the U.K. and beyond. The New Wave movies had little in common apart from a freshness of style that emanated from technical advances in film-making: highly mobile outdoor shooting, and indoor shooting at lower light levels made possible through more portable cameras and sound equipment, plus new high-speed film. As with so many artistic movements technology led the way, permitting creative forces to find a new means of expression.

☆ $800–1,000
☆ £525–675

▲ *Jules et Jim* (1961), Truffaut's third film, honors Jean Renoir – a director who had a major influence on his critical writings. The film was a lyrical riff on the bohemian lifestyle of the early 20th century. Its powerful score by Georges Delerue, combined with Raoul Coutard's cinematography, created a matrix of mood shifts between whimsy and pathos that set the stage for Jeanne Moreau's bravura performance. The Italian *due* (top) is a 1969 re-release and perfectly captures the film's atmosphere, while the original-release French *grande* by Broutin is a classic of modern poster art. The re-releases typically drop a color each time and the image becomes progressively paler.

▼ Marcel Camus' *Orfeu Negro* (*Black Orpheus*) is a prime example of a film that got caught up in the New Wave publicity machine. Camus had nothing in common with the other young French directors, but his film was at Cannes, he was a new name, and the press loves to cite as many examples as possible to justify their tag lines. Setting the Orpheus legend in Rio during Carnival, the film has a relentless power aided by a deafening Samba-driven score and some clever but still conventional photography. Georges Allard's *grande* for the 1960 release is a decorative favorite.

▲ Jean-Luc Godard burst upon the world of cinema with the New Wave and, ever the iconoclast in what was already a non-conformist movement, went on to be one of the few film-makers to consistently make movies exactly as he wanted them made. Each seems like a piece of an unfinished mosaic that, when completed, will form a singular vision of the world as an endless movie. The French *grande* for the 1963 original release of *Les Carabiniers* (*The Riflemen*) is by Jean Barnoux. Its patchwork imagery and saturated color fields echo the film's chaotic narrative of two mindless thugs pillaging the world, intercut with archival footage of warfare.

◄ Often considered the ultimate New Wave film, *A Bout de Souffle* (*Breathless*) appeared in 1959 and changed the way movies were made. It epitomized the freedom granted by the new equipment that had actually been developed by documentary film makers. But instead of recording factual imagery, Godard created a world of film noir gone mad. Calling on a cascade of memories culled from the thousands of films he had watched at Les Cinémathèque Français, he enshrined the jump cut as cinematic device. Clément Hurrell's *petite* poster for the original release shows lovers in a death grip of passion. Its ambivalent orientation is no less upside down, backwards, or sideways than the film.

★ $300–400

★ £200–275

★ $200–300

★ £125–200

▲ The American distribution rights for Truffaut's autobiographical first film, *Les 400 Coups*, were bought before the film won its prize at Cannes, and, judging by the tag line and imagery on the one-sheet, the U.S. distributor thought he had a great juvenile delinquent film on his hands. A whole new, and much duller, campaign began when what had been picked up as a cheap program-filler became a major art film. The French *grande* (right) for the 1968 re-release is considered the film's best paper since it captures one of the great moments in modern cinema – the freeze frame used as the last shot – but the 1959 original-release *grande* is still more valuable.

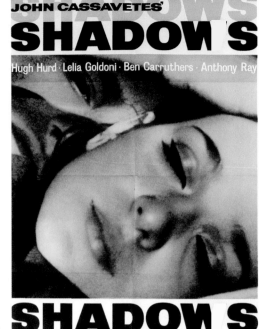

In the U.S. the "New Cinema," as it was called, produced limited-release, experimental films, such as Kenneth Anger's *Scorpin Rising*, Jonas Mekas' *Guns of the Trees*, and Robert Frank's *Pull My Daisy*. All benefited from new technology, but tended to be on the dull edge of the avant-garde and now seem dated and difficult. The films proved influential, inspiring the work of Andy Warhol and Paul Morrissey, who in turn gave a whole generation of film-makers a licence to make boring movies. Poster art for these titles is beyond scarce since very little was printed, most of the advertising being done in one-of-a-kind photographic blowups. John Cassavetes' *Shadows* (actually shot on 16mm film) was re-edited and fitted up for a 1960 commercial release, hence this U.S. one-sheet.

☆ $600–800
☆ £400–525

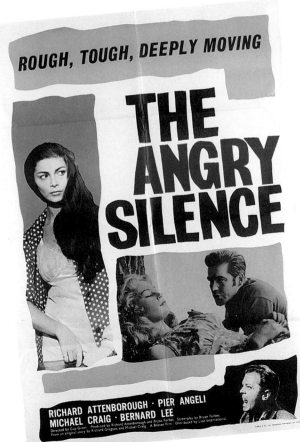

◀ Counterparts to the French New Wave were found chiefly in Britain, where a group of writers known as the "angry young men" found apt collaborators in such directors as Tony Richardson (*Look Back in Anger*, *The Loneliness of the Long Distance Runner*), Jack Clayton (*Room at the Top*), and Kerl Reisz (*Saturday Night and Sunday Morning*). Such films, appearing over a three-year period, made a sharp break with the post-war era of British film-making. Guy Green's 1960 *The Angry Silence* was a searing exposé of the "I'm All Right Jack" culture of the labor movement. This poster is typical of the U.S. one-sheets for this genre: the design is undistinguished and the values are minimal. The British quads for these titles are more desirable.

☆ $40–50
☆ £25–35

# Foreign Posters of U.S. Films

A minor joy of traveling is finding amusing indications of how other cultures view one's native land, and foreign movie art often offers interesting clues to such perceptions. French and Italian tourists are sometimes baffled by how their films are promoted in the U.S. or Britain but, conversely, American and British travelers can be at a loss to guess even the name of a film by simply looking at the graphic images displayed across the front of European movie theaters. While the huge publicity, promotion, and advertising departments at the majors would design a unified selling plan for a film, it was not unusual for something to get lost in the translation. This is a less common occurrence today, with the availability of high-speed communication, but in the days not so long ago when transatlantic calls had to be booked in advance and letterheads carried cable addresses, distance was a factor in changes to the images and text of posters. Also, cultural differences and language anomalies would prompt altered versions, and then there were certain countries that ignored the U.S. campaign altogether and produced an entirely new look for the promotion of the film in their country.

☆ $400–600
☆ £275–400

▲ The U.S. poster art for the 1959 release of *The Nun's Story* did its level best to hide the fact that this was a movie about nuns – a typical problem when the beleaguered promotion department is at odds with the production side of the studio. The French releasing arm of Warner Brothers had no such qualms and assigned a master of that country's poster art, Jean Masci, to create what is considered film advertising's most beautiful graphic depiction of Audrey Hepburn in the title role.

☆ $300–500
☆ £200–325

▲ This 1981 French *grande* for *Mommie Dearest* is by Bertrand, designer of illustrations for the release of *Love in the Afternoon* and *Lady and the Tramp*. Once again this example outshines the vapid U.S. campaign. Shocking when it first appeared, the film has now become a camp classic, but judging from this poster the illustrator knew that all along. Arguments go back and forth as to whether this is a portrait of Faye Dunaway or an image of the "Queen of Wooden Hangers" herself, Joan Crawford. Either way, it is a chilling poster and a popular Mother's Day present.

☆ $100–200
☆ £65–125

◀ One is forced to conclude that poker isn't very popular in Germany, since this A1 poster from that country makes no allusion to the central theme of the 1965 Steve McQueen film, which is about a high-stakes card game. (The U.S. poster had no problem with showing McQueen dealing cards, and interestingly neither did the popular French *grande* for this title.) This ploy is reminiscent of the original release posters for *The Hustler*, which ignored the film's pool theme as potential box-office poison. Though not credited, the artwork is probably by Lutz Peltzer, one of the masters of German poster art. The smaller A1 size (23 × 33 in), used as a standard format in that country, created a design challenge that often resulted in dramatic illustrations.

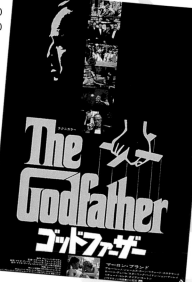

☆ $200–300
☆ £125–200

▶ This early 1970s Japanese poster is a major departure from the U.S. release one-sheet (a stark image of marionette strings and the title against a black background). The Japanese designer offered some relief by adding Brando's shadowy profile (an element from some of the European campaigns) and five scenes from the film. This is typical of Japanese posters, which are often slavish to the original design theme but add original and subtle touches that make them popular collectibles.

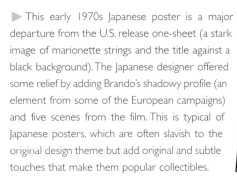

◀ The headline "Enjoy Once Again," the post-1970 audience code (NRC), and the modern logo treatment for United Artists all give it away – even an inexperienced collector should know that this Australian daybill is a re-issue, probably dating from the late '70s. More interesting is the use of several major elements from the original 1941 campaign that so strongly evoke the film's popular mystique. Before the days of home-video viewing classic films were watched in theaters dedicated to revivals. Obviously this poster was intended for such a cinema, seeking to rekindle memories of a favorite film. This kind of promotion was very seldom used in the U.S. or U.K., where resourceful owners of small theaters had to create their own promotional material to decorate their lobbies and house fronts.

☆ $50–75
☆ £35–50

☆ $800–1,000
☆ £525–675

◀ When this Belgian poster for *The Big Sleep* was consigned to a movie-poster sale at a New York auction house a few years ago, it took three experts to verify that it was not only authentic, but also an original release. Belgian posters are a quagmire for collectors, as films were often re-released with little overt indication on the poster. Tax stamps, printers' names and location, and paper quality provide important clues, as do paper sizes: pre-1940 Belgian posters (very rare) were usually close to A1 (23 x 33 in); during the war sizes varied because of paper shortages; the post-war size, as with this 1946–7 example, settled at 14 x18 in, then gradually expanded to roughly 14 x 22 in.

☆ $1,500–1,800
☆ £1,000–1,200

☆ $800–1,000
☆ £525–675

▲ Stanley Kubrick demanded a major say in the marketing of his films and often drove his distributors to distraction with his suggestions. The original campaign for the 1968 release of *2001: A Space Odyssey* was relentlessly consistent worldwide, with two basic poster styles (the space wheel, and the astronauts), but this monolithic approach came unstuck in Poland. The then state-run distribution system had a stable of designers, almost all graduates of the world's only school of poster design. These artists would produce often bizarre, and now quite collectible, posters – such as this example by Wyetor Gorka – based on their own highly personal interpretations of the film's message.

▲ So oblique is the imagery on this late 1950s Czech poster for *The Seven Year Itch* that it could just as easily be for *Some Like It Hot* – both were directed by Billy Wilder and starred Marilyn Monroe. Czech design combined film promotion with artful posters, but there is not a huge flow of material and without supply there is no significant marketplace. There are a few dealers offering posters from once-obscure sources on the Internet, and major European cinema paper fairs in London and Paris (notably in Argentueil in January) present good opportunities for buyers.

▶ This Italian *locandino* for the 1968 Steve McQueen thriller *Bullitt* has two stories to tell. It is typical of the entire European campaign which, through the use of an outsized pointing gun, sold the film as a violent gangster drama. Surprisingly the U.S. advertising material was much more subdued, attempting to suggest a similarity to a recent McQueen success, *The Thomas Crown Affair*. The other interesting fact is about the artist, Tom Chantrell. Until a few years ago his name was unknown, but a determined dealer discovered him in semi-retirement and, through interviews and a review of his personal archive, created a list of his key art. Almost all were British quads for U.S. films, from *Star Wars* to *East of Eden*, but, as with *Bullitt*, the artwork spilled over on to the Continent and became the entire alternative "look" of that film's career.

▲ ▶ These are the German release posters for two U.S. films with artwork by two different well-known American illustrators. Obviously unhappy with the standard U.S. campaign the distributor, in an unusual move, eschewed the use of a native artist and reached into an obscure corner of the key art to come up with these two images. Bob Peak's *Apocalypse Now* (1979) poster is considered the strongest art on the title and is sharply different from his U.S. version, which shows helicopters coming out of a sunset (though one edition does have a looming image of Brando, almost hidden in the clouds). Richard Amsel's 1970 *Woodstock* poster is far superior to the U.S. version, which was a series of photographs of the immense crowds at this event, geometrically arranged on a one-sheet as rows of lobby cards.

Black cinema reflects the racial divide that was prevalent within the movie industry, and the title of the seminal book on the theme, *A Separate Cinema*, by John Kisch, says it all. In the early part of the 20th century a thriving African-American film industry turned out so-called "race films" for a group of theaters created specifically to show nothing else, but the appearance of blacks in mainstream Hollywood films was limited to the stereotyped roles of porters or cooks, until the advent of sound. It seems that Al Jolson singing in black face introduced a whole new attitude, and several of the first talking films featured black performers. There were two major forces in early black cinema: the prolific and forceful producer, director, and writer Oscar Micheaux, who between 1918 and the 1940s made over 40 feature films; and the towering genius Paul Robeson, who devoted a good part of his career to making major films he knew were destined for a limited distribution. Hollywood co-opted some of the best talents and themes of independent black cinema in the "blaxploitation" movement of the 1970s. Recent film-makers such as Spike Lee have rekindled the Micheaux/Robeson tradition by creating an equal cinema.

▼ This 1936 film *Temptation* was an attempt by Oscar Micheaux to create in black cinema a parallel to certain Hollywood trends. Jean Harlow's steamy melodramas were at the height of popularity and this film was an imitation of the genre. The promotion sold Ethel Moses as "the negro Harlow" and her co-star, Lorenzo Tucker, as "the black Valentino." The movie had a budget of $15,000, much of which would have been spent on prints and advertising. The surviving examples of black cinema poster art indicate that the producers did not stint on the quality of design and printing, which makes them highly desirable, but these early posters are frustratingly hard to find.

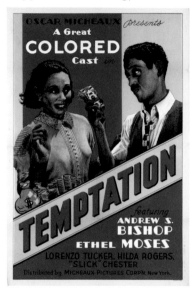

☆ $4,000–5,000
☆ £2,675–3,325

☆ $3,000–4,000
☆ £2,000–2,675

▲ When this 1935 window card appeared in a Boston poster sale a few years ago, a major dealer in black cinema ephemera, unwilling to risk the sometimes unreliable phone bidding system, flew in from New York to buy this one lot. Although in poor condition it is the only known copy of this format on the title, and the artwork is far different from the equally rare one-sheet. The film is a prime example of Oscar Micheaux's work; while he wrote and directed it his wife, A. Burton Russell, was the producer. Filmed under the title *Lem Hawkins' Confession*, the film vanished until 1983, when it was found in a Texas warehouse as one of 30 prints of major black-cast movies.

☆ $18,000–20,000
☆ £12,000–13,325

☆ $50–60
☆ £35–40

◀ Paul Robeson is a collectible unto himself: world-class athlete, attorney, author, noted public speaker, singer, and perhaps one of the 20th century's greatest actors. *Emperor Jones* was filmed in one week on a budget of $10,000, and while this isn't the first poster to be worth more than the filming cost, it may be the most famous. The few copies of the 1933 one-sheet that have appeared on the market have been absorbed into private collections, so the guide price is only an estimate. But with major institutions now buying black material, this might be just an opening bid.

▲ Spike Lee is outspoken about the scourge of racism and his movies consistently say the right thing, but he also loves to entertain as well as preach. A perfect mix of both elements, *Bamboozled* (2000) is a vicious contemporary satire on the minstrel tradition of black face, and this carried through to the advertising. The posters caused quite a controversy when issued and are well on their way to becoming collectible classics. This one-sheet, based on a turn-of-the-century advertising poster, shows the black leads in black face; the original artwork came from Lee's large collection of African-American memorabilia.

☆ $100–200
☆ £65–125

☆ $800–1,000
☆ £525–675

▲ There is a good supply of posters from the 1970s blaxploitation era, and several well-researched books to help identify those available and the artists who created them. This 1972 *Shaft's Big Score* half-sheet was designed by John Solie, who created a number of graphics in this genre. The *Shaft* movies were the most popular commercial films of the period and, for a brief and not too shining moment, it seemed as if "separate cinema" was coming back. However, what emerged was a group of well-made films great for retrospectives and poster collecting.

◀ The all-black-cast film of *Porgy and Bess* was a box-office flop when it appeared in 1959, but not for lack of promotion or advertising as a large number of U.S. one-sheets exist that routinely trade in the $400 range. This original-release German poster has a certain câché with collectors because of the artwork by Bruno Rehak, which rang some dramatic changes on the U.S. key art. The poster states the film is in the CinemaScope widescreen ratio, which indicates in Germany that it was being shown in "one-sheet" format, but in fact it was made in Todd-AO.

The urge to make drawings appear to move has been traced back to the dawn of history, when cave drawings showed animals with multiple legs, as if to illustrate them in motion. Mechanical animation, via such devices as the Zoetrope, developed far ahead of motion pictures, but it was almost a decade into film history, in 1906, that the first known animated film was made. Cartoons became part of each movie program during the silent era, but it wasn't until the introduction of sound and the emergence of the talents of Walt Disney that animated films came into their own. Collecting animation today basically means collecting Disney. While there are examples from other studios and creators, he so dominated the field that to collect non-Disney material is almost a conceit. There is barely any printed material to be found for pre-sound cartoons, and very little for the earliest Disney animations. A one-sheet for *Steamboat Willie*, for example, has long been the animation collector's Holy Grail, and the acquisition of material on *The Three Little Pigs* or the *Silly Symphony* series should be left to those with no limit on their credit cards.

☆ $2,000–3,000
☆ £1,325–2,000

▲ *Snow White and the Seven Dwarfs* (1937) was the first sound-era feature-length animated film and its massive popularity, and the scale of Disney's achievement, caught everyone unawares. This poster is the basic style A original release, which was re-struck several times as it rolled out through the distribution system. It looked like the film was to play forever, and several additional posters were created in styles B and C. These were printed in smaller quantities and command higher prices than the A version.

☆ $1,200–1,400
☆ £800–925

◄ One-sheets for cartoon shorts are not common. By 1946, the release year of this MGM Tom and Jerry cartoon, going to the movies was a time-consuming event: there were usually two full-length features, a newsreel, a humorous short, and a cartoon. All of these competed for promotion space in the lobby and the animated film usually got short shrift. Collecting posters for cartoons is often an ancillary to the hobby of collecting production cells from the films: they can offer an insight into the animators' craft as they re-work their images into the larger format.

◄ When *Sleeping Beauty* was released in 1959 it was Disney's most expensive feature. It was filmed using Super Technirama 70 – one of many new wide-screen formats created to lure people away from their TVs. This British quad emphasized the fairy-tale aspect of the myth, as opposed to the U.S. campaign, which opted for a bucolic/romantic image. The Disney publicity machine was expert at devising different campaigns for different countries. While income from foreign releases was tiny compared to the massive U.S. grosses, Walt Disney was conscious that he was building a worldwide franchise.

► Despite its clever blend of animation and live action, which was a great success, and its Oscar for Best Song with "Zip-A-Dee-Doo-Dah," *Song of the South* (1946) is now a non-film as far as Disney is concerned. To blame is the supposed portrayal of African-Americans as happy-go-lucky stereotypes, forever singing as they work. Actually the film emphasizes instead the fantasy world of Joel Chandler Harris and the creatures he created. This is evident in the 1956 British quad, which is as reasonably priced as most paper on this title – even that from the original release.

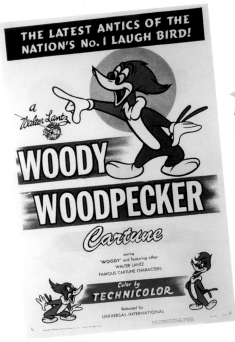

◄ Once a studio had created a popular cartoon character they put out a stock poster, as with this 1950 one-sheet. A theater could hold on to it for several years, popping it into a lobby display whenever they booked a film featuring that animated creature. Woody Woodpecker was the star of Universal Studios and was created by their lead animator, Walter Lantz, who started drawing cartoons in the silent era and was still working in the 1980s. One would assume that, since they were not tied to one film, stock posters would be readily available, but this is not the case. Not only were they retained by the theater, but the same poster was re-used over and over again until it was unusable.

◀ This French *grande* is from the original 1955 release of *Lady and the Tramp*, but the imagery is quite different from the U.S. release. In later releases this popular spaghetti-eating scene has invariably been used, usually with the two dogs accidentally kissing as they share a strand of pasta. Disney would often reach out and grab back ideas that had been generated during the creation of foreign campaigns. This was Disney's first feature in CinemaScope and, while perennially popular, the posters, except for three- and six-sheets, have trouble struggling above the $1,000 (£675) mark. Often re-issues fetch higher prices than initial versions, the more finely honed illustrations capturing the film's endearing qualities.

▶ Ralph Bakshi is a talented animator who, over the years, has created a solid body of work that is full of new techniques and innovations, especially concerning the blending of animation and live action; *Cool World*, whose 1992 one-sheet is illustrated here, is such a film. But he is also an example of Disney as the animation-collecting widow-maker. Not even the poster for this director's controversial *Coonskin* (1975) can reach the $100 mark, and the only reason the advertising art on *Wizards* (1977) sells for close to that is because the rock band The Grateful Dead objected to the use of their logo and asked for it to be withdrawn.

► One-sheets for post-1960 shorts were sometimes issued, but a half-sheet is very unusual. It implies that there was a full range of paper put out on the title, but no one has ever found a six-sheet for *The Critic*, a brilliant 1963 film that runs but a few minutes. It features the voice of Mel Brooks as an old man who wanders into a theater showing an experimental short. While animator Ernie Pintoff visually skewers the entire 1960s genre of abstract films, Brooks supplies a hysterical running commentary. No doubt Pintoff, who came to cartoons via graphic design, created this poster.

★ $200–300
★ £125–200

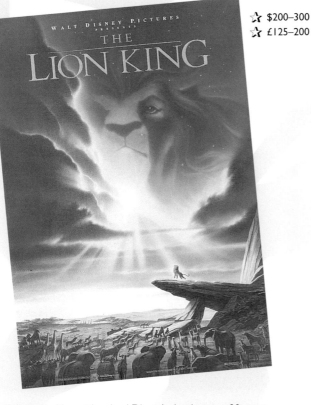

★ $200–300
★ £125–200

▼ For a few brief shining moments it looked as though the much-missed tradition of a cartoon short preceding a feature was to return. *Dick Tracy* (1990) had a brilliant short, *Rollercoaster Rabbit*, accompanying it into theaters, and *Honey I Shrunk The Kids*, from the next year, was teamed with *Tummy Trouble*, which, like the earlier short, had its own one-sheet. But it was not to be. No doubt Disney could have turned out an endless number of mini-movies, but they would have had to compromise on quality since the cost of the first two was stratospheric. Posters for both shorts sell in the same range, and they would make an interesting pair to collect.

▲ If *The Little Mermaid* revived Disney's dominance of feature animation (see p.55), its 1994 film *The Lion King* turned it into a dictatorship. The phenomenal success of this movie has spawned best-selling books, a highly rated TV series, platinum records, and a Broadway show that is eternally sold out. The posters have been escalating in price, and it is indicative of the specialized nature of collecting animated paper that they have gone higher, especially in light of the restrictions Disney places on their use. Technically, original movie posters should be returned to the distributor or destroyed, and Disney can be quite strict with theaters about this.

★ $80–100
★ £55–65

Although there are rare exceptions studios would usually create scene cards like these only for animated features (most shorts would have reusable cards, similar to stock posters), and even then they were not issued in any great quantity. Collectors are fond of this format because it echoes the actual animation cells used in the production of the film and the smaller size seems to give a more intense tone to the image. The two cards illustrated, from the original release of *Snow White*, display the usual price disparity created by auctions. Cards from this film don't appear on the market very often, and the last time a complete set of eight was offered in 1999 it sold for close to $10,000 (£6,675).

☆ $1,600–1,800
☆ £1,075–1,200

☆ $600–800
☆ £400–525

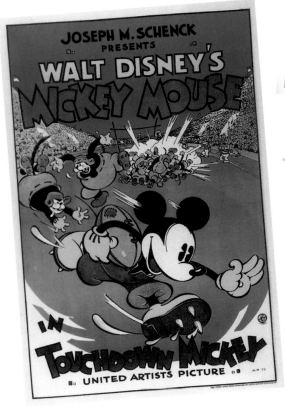

With this one-sheet for the 1932 release of *Touchdown Mickey* collectors enter a rarefied world. It is thought to be the only one to exist, and while all pre-*Snow White* Disney posters are valuable, especially those with a sports theme, the superior graphic design of this one makes it even more desirable. The October 2000 U.S. auction at which this poster achieved its record price consisted of the entire holdings of one man who was relentless in his pursuit of the best early Disney paper, forcing other bidders into different areas of collecting. When he came to sell, the market was bereft of major collectors and only a few stellar examples, such as this, fared well.

☆ $75,000–80,000
☆ £50,000–53,350

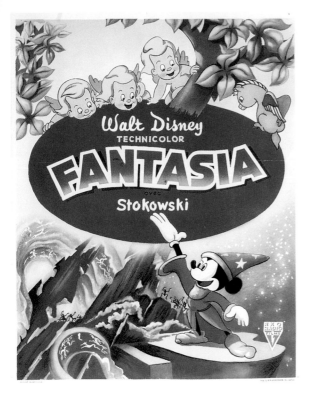

⭐ $300–400
⭐ £200–275

◀ Designed as an attempt to marry classical music and animation, *Fantasia* did not meet with great success on its original 1940 release. But it has proven to be an animated annuity – its numerous re-releases growing more popular with each new generation. This original Belgian post-war release poster is an affordable introduction to the expensive paper on this title. The combination of Mickey, the would-be magician from the *Sorcerer's Apprentice* sequence, with the putti created to animate Beethoven's *Sixth Symphony*, is unique among European imagery. The 1970 re-release poster was heavily influenced by late 1960s psychedelia.

▶ From 1950 on the creation of animated features was no longer a major focus of Disney studios. They branched out into TV (with the Mickey Mouse Club), amusement parks, and live-action movies. By the 1980s the animation department was almost non-existent, until new management was brought in and a strong commitment was made to new major works. *The Little Mermaid* was released in 1989, for which this one-sheet was made, and was a huge success; there is now a steady flow of films. Disney was one of the first studios to use double-sided posters (to take advantage of the new backlit showcases), and they sell at a premium over the single-sided examples. As more theaters install lightboxes, single-sided posters for major releases will gradually disappear.

⭐ $100–200
⭐ £65–125

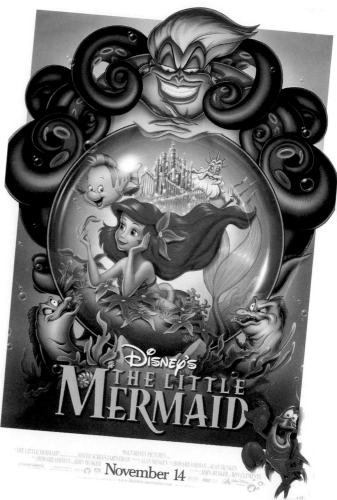

# Musicals

The film musical was an American creation and its popularity was limited to its home-grown audience, with occasional success in other English-speaking countries such as Britain, Canada, and Australia. During the golden years, the early '30s through the mid-'50s, musicals were popular enough for the studios to ignore the foreign market (where films often had the musical numbers removed because audiences found characters bursting into song at any moment unrealistic). However, after this period they slowly declined in popularity in the U.S. – production costs rose and non-domestic grosses became a larger part of a film's income, so fewer were made. A handful of Broadway hits were turned into films post-1960, among them *My Fair Lady*, which was a hit, and *A Chorus Line*, which was not. Meanwhile a small group of films with a pop music, rock-'n'-roll soundtrack kept the genre, if not the tradition, alive. What has thrived among collectors is a strong interest in any memorabilia associated with the great musicals. Just as the soundtracks live on, the films themselves are forever being revived, thus constantly creating a new audience for any ephemera, especially posters, associated with the great song-and-dance films of the past.

▼ Neophyte poster dealers invariably snap up every Elvis film poster that comes their way, assuming there is a vast market for anything related to Presley's career. It comes as a hard lesson that not all Elvis posters are created equal and there are many dealers with non-movers permanently in their inventory, such as lobby displays for *Charro!*, *Change of Habit*, and *Clambake*. In reality only a handful of posters for the 33 films Elvis starred in are highly collectible. This 1957 one-sheet for *Jailhouse Rock* is one, as are posters for *Love Me Tender*, *Blue Hawaii*, and *Viva Las Vegas*.

☆ $1,500–2,000
☆ £1,000–1,325

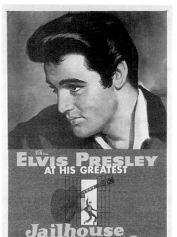

☆ $800–1,000
☆ £525–675

▲ Arthur Freed, producer of *An American in Paris*, began his career as a lyricist at MGM in 1929 and worked his way up. By the 1940s he had his own production team, the Freed Unit. It turned out hit after hit and was home to such directors as Busby Berkeley, Stanley Donen, and Vincente Minnelli, creator of this Gene Kelly vehicle. As the movie won Best Picture in 1951 the poster fetches a respectable price, but the design, for a film that so lavishly explored the world of Parisian art, lacks imagination.

☆ $25,000–30,000
☆ £16,675–20,000

▶ A great movie, with perhaps the most striking and innovative poster of any film, this one has it all. The one-sheet (right) from 1933 has appeared on the market just twice, and it is thought there is only one other copy in existence. It is its graphic power that drives the price; the ancillary paper has not the same value, as lobby cards have sold for a relatively cheap $2,000, press books $300, and heralds $200–300. The exception is a mini window card which, for a poster in this price range, should sell for a few hundred dollars. It went for $4,000 at auction, mainly because it displays the same image as the full poster.

☆ $800–1,000
☆ £525–675

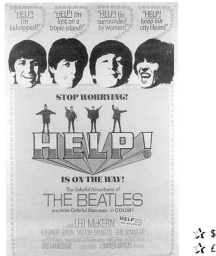

▲ One tends to forget that Audrey Hepburn was a dancer until considering *Funny Face*, which came along in 1957. Her performance was dazzling and the whole film is a visual and musical treat. Fred Astaire gave a performance worthy of his best '30s hits and Stanley Donen's direction was impeccable. All of these factors have created a group of collectors eager for material, and almost anything from this title is worth pursuing. The full set of lobby cards sells close to the value of the poster, and there are several much sought-after foreign versions, especially the French *grande* (with the title *Drôle de Frimousse*). Even the 1964 re-release poster has sold as high as $600.

☆ $600–800
☆ £400–525

▲ The Beatles' 1964 feature, *A Hard Day's Night*, has a rather vapid poster but it sells for over $1,000 because people love the movie and it was a first screen appearance. The 1965 one sheet for *Help!* is a much better graphic but the film did not receive the same acclaim, and with musicals that affects the price (posters with great graphics may be passed at auction if the film itself is not rated). The bizarre prices paid for Fab Four memorabilia do not extend to movie posters, in which Beatles collectors show little interest.

☆ $1,800–2,000
☆ £1,200–1,325

▶ Perhaps the best musical produced by the Arthur Freed unit at MGM, *Singin' In The Rain* is another in a long series of films that create a biography of Hollywood. In this case the premise is the transition from the silent to the sound era, but the story, as with so many pre-1960 musicals, is just a vehicle for a cavalcade of outstanding numbers. The title scene is one of the most famous film clips of all time and should have been the poster image, but that would have excluded the other stars. (Such considerations are responsible for many mediocre images.) This 1952 one-sheet would sell for a lot more if it truly captured the mood of this near-perfect musical.

☆ $400–600
☆ £275–400

☆ $800–1,000
☆ £525–675

▲ After *Help!*, the Beatles owed United Artists one more picture on their three-film contract, but no longer wished to give up several months of their then very complicated lives to shoot a movie. Animation allowed them to have very little to do with the production of the film, although they liked the rough cut so much they agreed to shoot the short live bit at the end. The 1968 film has become a cathedral of myths: American pop illustrator Peter Max is often credited with the look of the film and its poster art, but it was in fact the creation of U.K. animator, John Williams. The U.S. one-sheet on the right is the basic image of the campaign, but the Italian *due* ("antipasto on an acid trip") is a favorite.

⭐ $500–700
⭐ £325–475

◀ The glowing Cecil Beaton photo of Audrey Hepburn would be reason enough to display this Italian *due* for *My Fair Lady*, but its interest lies in the fact that it dates from a 1975 re-release. It is difficult to spot Italian re-issues, but the clue here is the W incorporating a 7 (Warner Bros./Seven Arts) at the lower left. This is an image change for Warner (from the WB in a shield) that took place in the early 1970s, when most of the majors went through a fit of updating their classic identification images. Leo, the MGM lion, became just a shadow of himself in the late '60s, while United Artists morphed into TransAmerican.

⭐ $80–100
⭐ £50–65

▶ This 1972 Billie Holiday bio turned out to be a bit of a soap opera, but the French *grande* picks up on the film's underlying power. Diana Ross, in her first acting role, brilliantly conveys the effect of drug addiction on the great jazz singer's life and career. The film's themes are echoed in the imagery (the handcuffs, emphasizing the white flower) and the "fade away" effect harks back to the '20s. The blues and indigos are perfect '70s touches and large format further empowers the design. Here is a poster that is affordable but might well prove to have a long life as a collectible.

⭐ $300–500
⭐ £200–325

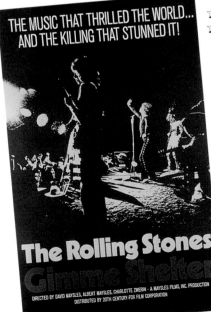

◀ The rock-concert film became a staple on the release schedule of every major distributor. Cheap to make, it had a built-in audience of fans for the starring group. This 1970 Rolling Stones film was a major variant. Created by the cinema vérité documentary team of David and Albert Maysles, it filmed not just the concert at Altamont but also the chilling chaos and murder that ensued. Performing some of their best songs, the Stones are captured in a mood of fan-induced ecstasy that devolves into horror at what occurs. This one-sheet solarizes an actual frame from the film and the blatant headline says it all – Hollywood co-opting even murder to sell a movie.

# Academy Award Winners

☆ $200–300
☆ £135–200

When the massive popularity of television was ravaging Hollywood in the early 1950s, studios banned TV sets from the offices and dressing rooms on their production lots. Now, as another example of how the L.A. dream masters can turn adversity into gold, one billion people tune in to watch the annual Oscar ceremony, which is actually over three hours of publicity for films that for the most part are, by some strange coincidence, still in release on the night of the telecast. The golden statuettes given out by the Academy have inspired an entire group of collectors who attempt to acquire an example of advertising from each of the Best Picture winners since *Wings* won in 1927. Foremost among this collecting group is the Academy itself, which has been trying to obtain an original year-of-release one-sheet for each of these films. Several years ago, after a long search, it discovered the poster for *Grand Hotel* (1932) – the only copy known to exist – and it now has only to find one, for *Cavalcade* (1933), to complete the collection. Most collectors are satisfied with alternative formats, such as lobby cards or inserts, for such hard-to-find titles, but they too can be stymied when they try to complete their set with material from such expensive titles as *All Quiet on the Western Front* and *Casablanca*.

▲ While lobby cards on this 1945 film, *The Informer*, are relatively easy to come by, the one-sheet is scarce and therefore quite pricey (over $4,000), so this dramatic scene card is a good alternative. The avant-garde type style used to splash the title across the card is unusual, and gives the cards from this set an added desirability as examples of new trends in movie promotion design. The movie took Oscars for McLaglen's performance and John Ford's direction, as well as for script and score.

☆ $2,000–2,400
☆ £1,300–1,600

▲ A classic film, an unusual aspect, and a rare format give this landscape jumbo lobby card from *It Happened One Night* a high price tag. Even a lowly herald for this 1934 title sells for several hundred dollars and the one-sheets go for over $30,000. Adding to the cachet of this particular lobby display is the lush lithography, and its presentation on textured cartridge paper. The film was the first to sweep the top five Oscar categories, and also perhaps the first to use the Academy Awards as a marketing tool, mentioning them in all advertising after the presentation.

☆ $2,000–3,000
☆ £1,350–2,000

☆ $80–100
☆ £55–65

▲ In 1947 the Academy recognized foreign-language films by according them their own category, thereby opening endless debate over what films can be nominated, who nominates them, and who gets to vote. Federico Fellini, who won this prize three times with *La Strada*, *8½*, and *Amarcord*, is represented here by a 1974 British quad. Academy Award collectors tend to ignore this category, as attempts to accumulate one of each winning title are thwarted by the expense of some early examples and the almost total lack of any material for some of the truly obscure films.

☆ $400–500
☆ £275–325

▲ When *Lawrence of Arabia* was released in 1962 Columbia knew it had a winner, and poured out tons of advertising material. It opened as a limited engagement roadshow, for which a whole campaign was devised, followed by another for the general release and yet others when it won 11 Academy Awards. All the campaigns had A, B, and C styles, and everything was produced in all size formats. The film proved just as successful in Europe. The French *grande* by George Kerfyser illustrated here is popular, and there is another style in this size that also brings high prices. Each re-release has brought with it new, sometimes stunning images.

◄ This 1961 re-release three-sheet is a modestly priced entry into the world of mega-priced Academy-Award-winner posters. The original-release 1939 three-sheet has sold as high as $29,000, which gives one an idea of what the other paper on the film from that year goes for. *Gone with the Wind* won nine Academy Awards and most likely would have swept every category had not *Stagecoach*, *Mr. Smith Goes to Washington*, *Beau Geste*, *Wuthering Heights*, *Ninotchka*, *Goodbye Mr. Chips*, and *The Wizard of Oz* also appeared that year. There are collectors who limit themselves to the plethora of material produced for this film, some of whom have established their own private museums.

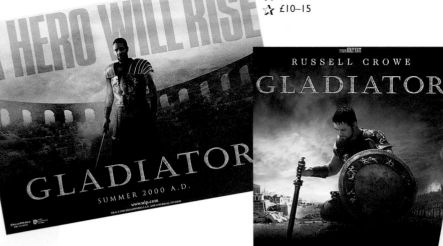

☆ $15–20
☆ £10–15

☆ $30–40
☆ £20–25

RIDLEY SCOTT

RUSSELL CROWE

GLADIATOR

L'esclave qui défia l'Empire.

www.gladiator-the-film.com

RIDLEY SCOTT

RUSSELL CROWE

GLADIATOR

MAY 5. 2000 A.D.
www.gladiator-the.film.com

☆ $20–30
☆ £15–20

▲ While one assumes *Gladiator* (2000) is a typical Best Picture, only one other such epic has won the award (*Ben Hur* in 1959). Instead it joins a list of immensely popular but swiftly forgotten winners, such as *Cimarron* (1931) and *The Greatest Show on Earth* (1952). Just as the nominating ballots are being mailed, the studios wage intense publicity campaigns and trade papers and billboards display lavish ads. The three posters shown are all minis: on the left is the British lobby give-away poster, with the powerful tag line, "A Hero Will Rise"; the center French *affichette* shows the dramatic image used in the Continental campaign; and the small poster on the right is one of a series created for the U.S. release.

☆ $800–1,000
☆ £525–675

◀ Pictured is a set of member ballots from 1944 for the 17th Annual Academy Awards. The 13 crafts nominate among their own, except for the Best Picture which is open to all, and then the entire membership votes on those nominations. This package consists of the first round of craft nominations for the actor's category, the second round of ballots for the five best in each category, a list of titles eligible for Best Picture, screening information, and a pair of serially numbered envelopes for each set of votes, to be returned to the accounting firm of Price, Waterhouse & Co.

$80–100
£55–65

$200–300
£125–200

*The Bridge on the River Kwai* won seven Oscars in 1957 and it might have won eight if the Academy had known that Michael Wilson and Carl Foreman had written the screenplay, but the men had been blacklisted in the anti-communist hysteria of the time. The credit went to Pierre Boule, who wrote the original novel but could not speak English. The history of the Oscars is rife with such anomalies: actors with a starring role will engineer a nomination as Best Support to boost their chances of winning. This style A half-sheet is part of an alternative campaign attempting to sell *Kwai* as an action/war movie.

$400–600
£275–400

The U.S. one-sheet for *The Godfather* (1972), done in stark white on black and picturing marionette strings, has never been very popular with collectors. It does not really capture the mood of this powerful film, which won three Oscars. The gap has been filled by foreign versions, chief among them the Italian poster and this U.K. one-sheet. They appear in a rare format, one inch shorter than the U.S. posters of the time, and were issued for only a handful of releases. Stills are quite desirable, especially the "family" wedding photo and any pictures of the baptism scene that, crucially for collectors, identifies the baby as Coppola's daughter, Sofia.

The success of this 1976 film has as much to do with the artful publicity campaign surrounding its creation as it does with the down-and-out boxer winning against all odds. The U.S. one-sheet illustrated is the basic building block of any *Rocky* collection, but each film's campaign was quite distinct so there exists an ample supply of interesting material. Perhaps the most valuable of the *Rocky* posters is the Fight Style from the second film, which simulates an old-fashioned boxing announcement heralding "The Rematch of The Century: Rocky Balboa Vs. Apollo Creed"; this example of clever film promotion, in yellow and black, sells in the $600 to $800 range. The four sequels have created an entire sub-culture of *Rocky* movie collectibles.

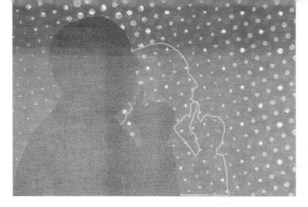

# Hitchcock

French film critics have labored under a cloud ever since an obscure reviewer writing in an even more obscure 1950s film journal lavishly praised the directorial efforts of Jerry Lewis. This typical Gallic conceit has gained the status of an international myth, overshadowing a tradition of film analysis that offered major insights into the work of such masters as Alfred Hitchcock. The French love affair with "Hitch" was on a par with its obsession with "Charlot" (Charles Chaplin), engendering long and thoughtful articles in highbrow literary journals. While those in the English-speaking world attended Hitchcock films in droves, the French embraced not only the films but also the persona of this British director, whose movies contained labyrinths of deceit and myriad levels of mis-direction. This love affair reached its peak with the publication of François Truffaut's famed interviews. While the French introduced us to the inner workings of a bizarre mind, it was Hitchcock himself who herded us into theaters to view his work. He was a tireless, but very subtle, self-promoter, and he ran a school on movie PR for the publicity departments of the film studios that released his films.

▲ This 1973 re-release *grande* for *Secret Agent* says it all about the French and Hitchcock. From the 1950s he is invariably featured on posters for his films and, as in this case, often much more prominently than the star. Released in 1936 this thriller, loosely based on stories by Somerset Maugham, is considered a minor work, but is often a guilty pleasure for fans of this man, the paradigm of "director as auteur." Hitchcock's sub-text here is that the spying game is a fool's errand, with loyalty for sale and ineptness rampant.

▲ *I Confess* (1953) stars Montgomery Clift and Anne Baxter, but the real protagonists of the film are the Catholic Church's Seal of Confession and Quebec City. Hitchcock's Catholicism comes to the fore here: the twisted streets and looming architecture provide an ideal background to the conflict between reason and faith. This Argentine one-sheet is typical of posters from that country in that its artwork is unique. The designs can be striking, but their popularity and value is tempered by the huge number that have been imported to the U.S.A.

☆ $200–400
☆ £125–275

The original release insert, left, for *Rear Window* (1954) is a fairly conventional pastiche of the key art for the film, but the poster for the 1962 re-release, far left, features an image of Hitchcock. By this time, Hitchcock had become something of a celebrity through the wry and often morbid introductions he presented each week at the beginning of his highly rated weekly TV show. Of the film, many critics have stated the obvious: that Stewart is actually Hitchcock, observing through a camera the human drama unfolding on a giant screen. Some reviewers actually feel sympathy for Raymond Burr, and there have been movie audiences known to cheer when Stewart gets his other leg broken.

☆ $600–800
☆ £400–525

Although artists do not always get to see the films they are to promote, and often rely only on stills and a shooting script, it is fairly clear that Saul Bass, the designer of this insert for *Vertigo* (1958), had access to a print. His relentless orange/red, almost dayglo swirls are a bit muted here and, more importantly, reduced to half the image area. The rest is taken up with a moment of frozen passion – summing up Stewart's obsession and mental frailty. If a relationship can be sealed with a kiss, so can fate, and from this moment Stewart is in an endless spiral, captured in the artwork from the Bass key art.

☆ $800–1,000
☆ £525–675

☆ $900–1,200
☆ £600–800

"The Birds Is Coming" was one of the great movie tag lines, and again the studio used Hitchcock's image on advance posters and a series of giant billboards that were placed in every major city, causing hours of argument and media commentary on correct grammar. *The Birds* (1963) is Hitchcock at his most misanthropic, exposing the ways in which people create cages for each other, just as they do for the creatures who attack them. The scene in which Tippi Hedren is quietly sitting on a bench while birds gather behind her is perhaps Hitchcock's greatest few minutes of film. This is the U.S. three-sheet, considered the best art on what was visually a lack-luster campaign.

The greatest single force behind the collecting of film posters is the attraction of movie stars. All other categories, be they defined by genre, illustrator, printing, or design, pale in comparison to the almost illogical need to accumulate original movie paper relating to a favorite performer. While the collecting of ephemera connected to luminaries of the 19th-century stage was undoubtedly popular, the compulsion to hoard everything from scrapbooks to billboards was fostered by a combination of Hollywood's vast publicity machine and the unique bond that appears to develop in darkened theaters around the world between the huge images projected on to a screen and an audience lost in a world of dreams. This part of poster collecting seems to bypass generational barriers. Old films on television, the invention of the VCR, and the emergence of classic films on DVD have seen growing numbers of younger people become fixated with stars of the past. Louise Brooks has more fans now than she did during her career, and children of the baby-boomers quite often drop Bette Davis quotes into their conversation.

▼ In the early 1930s a craftsman on the MGM lot fell in love with *Grand Hotel*, the showcase film for MGM's galaxy of stars; he asked for a copy of the one-sheet and squirreled it away. When it was discovered and auctioned at the end of the century, the Academy, who had years before resolved to procure a poster for every Academy Award Best Picture, acquired this unique example for just under $50,000. There are thousands of films for which no posters survive, but only a handful of lost classics that command prices on this level.

☆ $50,000–60,000
☆ £33,350–40,000

☆ $4,000–5,000
☆ £2,675–3,325

▲ *Angel* was not a very successful film, but this 1937 one-sheet is high on the list of "must have" Marlene Dietrich collectibles due to Hans Flato's stunning artwork. Dietrich projected her beauty with a power only true stars possess, visually seducing famed photographers and movie cameramen alike, and this lithographic illustration is one of her most famous images. Certainly a mega-star in the '30s, she was elevated to a new level of adoration during the war when she performed for Allied troops, in battle conditions, just miles from the German front, despite the Nazis having placed a price on her head.

Elizabeth Taylor is among the most collectible of film stars, battling for first place with Marilyn Monroe and James Dean. This British quad for *Cat on a Hot Tin Roof* would garner nowhere near the quoted price range without her presence in the credits and the seductive image of her stretched out on the bed – still a bit daring in 1958. Her performance in *Cleopatra* (1963) elevated her to superstardom, and most material associated with this picture is desirable – especially some of the excellent high-quality Italian original-release posters. Having played host to the filming in Rome for so many years Italy felt a special fondness for this film and gave it a glorious send-off.

$400–500
£275–325

$3,000–4,000
£2,000–2,675

Jean Harlow started her career in Hal Roach comedy shorts. Her big break came when Howard Hughes, in the process of adding sound to his 1927 production of *Hell's Angels*, cast Harlow in the lead (to replace an actress with a heavy foreign accent.) She then played several roles as a platinum-blonde sexpot. As her career blossomed she developed into an excellent comedic actress – evident in the film *Hold Your Man* – and this 1933 lobby card is a classic Harlow collectible. Her death at a young age, combined with the sparse output of such a brief career, created a large devoted fan base.

$300–400
£200–275

Considered the ultimate screwball comedy, *Bringing Up Baby* left both critics and audiences dazed and confused when it opened in 1938, but it has gone on to become a popular favorite. It is one of the most modern of vintage films, as fresh and frantic today as it was then. Much credit for this goes to leading lady Katherine Hepburn, whose long, versatile, and Oscar-winning career has created a legion of fans. This one-sheet is among the most sought-after of 1930s posters. It combines child-like cartoon images with photo-montage, capturing the film's mood via the pre-war constructivist poster trend.

☆ $400–600
☆ £275–400

◀ Every major movie-poster auction has some inevitable categories: Bond, Hitchcock, horror and sci-fi, film noir, and classic silents are among the favorites. There is only one actress who gets her own group of lots (often running to several pages of entries) and that is Marilyn Monroe. She made just a dozen major films, but these generated enough material to keep hordes of collectors bidding. *Bus Stop* (1956), illustrated here by a half-sheet, was her first film under her new contract with Fox, which gave her more freedom over script and director. Her hard-won authority yielded perhaps her best-ever performance.

▶ While films about Hollywood had long been popular fare for U.S. film-makers, the Europeans had contributed little about their own industry until 1960. It was as if they had been saving up to make a major entry: *La Dolce Vita* was a searing commentary on the world of false glamor and fake glory (after all, it gave us the word "paparazzi" – actually the name of a famously aggressive news photographer). The image of Anita Ekberg and the kitten, used on this U.S. release 40 × 60, was one of several used in the Italian campaign, and it proved popular in the mass distribution the film received in North America. The Italian posters still fetch the highest price, but this example would come close if the releasing company hadn't produced such a massive amount of promotional material.

☆ $400–600
☆ £275–400

Most Orson Welles biographies claim he made *The Lady From Shanghai* to save his marriage to Rita Hayworth, but the film's arduous production schedule and poor reception only made things worse and the relationship ended soon after the movie's release in 1947. It is now regarded as one of his best films and holds a firm place in the film noir pantheon. This style A half-sheet is one of the few formats on the title to use a minor aspect of the key art. The style B in this size bears the same graphic elements as the one-sheet, and the more common tag line: "I told you... you know nothing about wickedness."

★ $1,200–1,400
★ £800–925

★ $400–500
★ £275–325

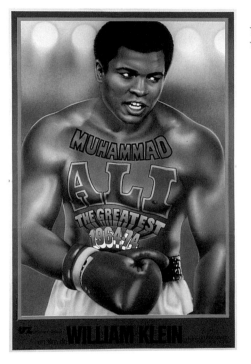

▼ Original release Marx Brothers movie paper is another casualty of popularity. Their films played for years during their first go-around and the posters ended in tatters. All pre-war Marx Brothers material is highly collectible and anything in excellent, unrestored condition is especially prized. Such is the case with this jumbo window card for *A Night at the Opera*, which has two factors influencing its value: it is a rare format in pristine condition; and another is yet to be found. The artwork for this 1935 film is credited to famed illustrator Al Hirschfeld, who produced a huge number of posters for MGM during this period.

▲ Collectibles connected with movies about sports are popular with fans, and baseball and boxing contribute most to the genre, which is largely made up of fictionalized biopics or melodramas starring a cast of Hollywood players. This 1974 French poster (in an odd size of 33 x 47 in) is for an unusual film about Muhammad Ali: *The Greatest*, directed by William Klein. Such is the force of Ali's personality that he dominates the film and turns it into a feature-length drama. At auctions the poster is grouped with sports images, but the fervid bidding from all quarters is a tell-tale sign of its graphic power.

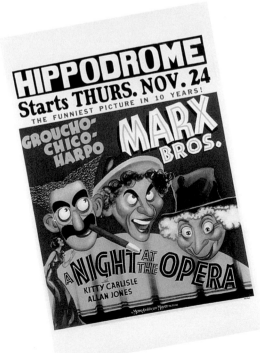

★ $2,000–3,000
★ £1,325–2,000

☆ $400–500
☆ £275–325

◀ This lobby card serves as a 14 x 11-in textbook for collectors, filled with warning signs and exceptions to the rule. Although it is a 1955 re-release (popular because it shows a good selection of the cast) it sells for the guide price of the 1939 release because it is signed by Olivier. Signed material is a constant problem: purist collectors are upset that someone has scribbled all over a treasure, while autograph collectors complain that the posters are too big to fit into their albums. Here the signature is discreet and the price is maintained by Olivier collectors, since he was a reluctant signer. Note the censor stamp – some places gave approval of the advertising as well as the film.

☆ $100–150
☆ £65–100

☆ $200–300
☆ £125–200

▲ The Quiet Man premiered in 1952 but it was in constant release for years, playing long runs and often being revived at local theaters in neighborhoods with a large Irish population. The constant booking of this John Wayne movie took its toll on the prints and advertising material, so Republic decided to re-release it in 1957. Republic was not a major and had to work to a smaller budget, using the same printing plates for all the poster art (including the six-sheet – not usually a re-release format) with a small "R57" slugged into the lower right-hand corner. Fans of this film and its posters (not necessarily movie-paper collectors) maintain the value of the re-issue material, as with this half-sheet that sells for almost as much as the one on display during the film's initial run.

▲ Gilda is one of movie-poster collecting's "mega titles." The original release one-sheet from 1946, featuring the famed illustration of Hayworth by Robert Coburn, routinely sells at auction for over $10,000 (£6,675), and the three-sheet, almost overpowering in the larger size, does even better. This window card is an example of "starter" paper on such a desirable film. It is in poor condition, with tape marks visible, and the printer did a sloppy job with the theater and dates, overlapping the tag line and leaving too much white space below. Add to this an unappealing graphic and its low price is inevitable.

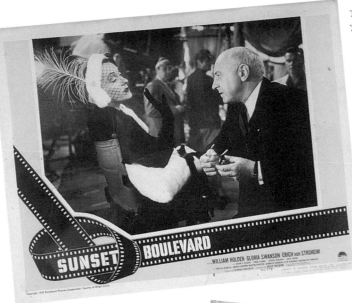

◀ Hollywood is often its own favorite topic, and *Sunset Boulevard* is regarded as one of the best in this reflective genre. It suffered from a poorly designed set of posters and larger accessory paper, and its mood of doom amidst faded fame was best captured in the lobby card set, which doesn't have a "dead" card in it. The one pictured shows Norma Desmond's visit to her old studio and features Gloria Swanson and Cecil B. De Mille playing himself, which wasn't too difficult since he spent the first 12 years of his career as a stage actor. Dating from the original release in 1950, the card's retro use of a border element (the ominous noose-like film strip) harks back to lobbies of the 1920s, the era when Norma Desmond was in her glory.

▲ Twentieth Century-Fox knew they had a powerful selling tool with this image. They used it on almost all formats for *The Seven Year Itch* (1955), from the insert through the 40 x 60 in, as well as this half-sheet. But for the one-sheet, the most important single piece of promotional paper for a movie, they created a strange illustration of Monroe hanging out of a window, holding a pair of shoes. Understandably, convention is here turned aside as the standard poster is much less valuable than this classic motif.

☆ $400–500
☆ £275–325

▶ The saga of the making of Orson Welles' *Othello* has been detailed in two books and is the subject of countless anecdotes. Little of its three years in production was spent shooting the film. Time and again the cast would be disbanded while Welles left to appear in films to earn money to complete the project. Despite such adversity the result is a masterpiece. This 1952 British quad pulls together several visual elements that were popular themes in posters from other countries. As the film was independently produced it had different distributors in all of the major markets, so there are widely varying styles on this title.

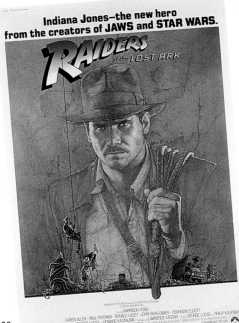

☆ $200–300
☆ £125–200

◀ ▼ Harrison Ford has not only been fortunate in his roles, but the posters associated with his movies have proven quite popular also. In this U.S. one-sheet (left) by Richard Amsel, the entire look of the poster perfectly reflects the "ripping yarns" atmosphere that Spielberg so successfully created on screen. As for the Polish poster by Jakbu Erol, one can only assume he saw a darker side to the film. The artwork brings to mind a horror film and until non-Polish speakers analyze the imagery and text, *Raiders Of The Lost Ark* does not leap to mind. It is a classic of the Warsaw school of poster art.

☆ $300–400
☆ £200–275

▶ Ridiculed at the time of its release in 1977 as a piece of disco spin-off fluff, it wasn't until the mid '90s that the power of retrospect revealed a film that perfectly encapsulated an era while at the same time told the story of urban youth wandering aimlessly in a world of flashing lights and recorded music. It was Fellini's *I Vitteloni* brought to the dance floor, and Travolta's performance is a joy. The one-sheet illustrated, with its oft-lampooned pose, and Travolta's deer-in-the-strobe-lights stare, is the advance. The regular release poster has the same image, with credits. The film was released with an R rating but the studio edited out the naughty bits to get an acceptable PG designation, and a new poster was issued. It cleverly refracts the same image into photo strips, as if the entire one-sheet was being reflected by the spinning disco ball, but it sells for less.

◀ Western posters are vastly popular, used to decorate more knotty-pine-paneled rec-rooms than any other genre, but Hollywood loved them also and produced thousands from the beginning of the silent period, such as *The Great Train Robbery* (1903). This vast output created acres of paper and it is only exceptional "oaters" (as *Variety* refers to them) that sell for a significant price. The 1933 one-sheet shown has excellent graphics, is an early sound-era example, and features the famous cowboy Tom Mix, but even with all those elements it struggles to sell for $1,000 (£675). No one should turn down a one-sheet for *The Searchers* (1956) or *Stagecoach* (1939), but collectors should be cautious when approaching this area.

# Auteurs

Defining a new way of looking at films, "Les Politiques des Auteurs" was developed in the pages of the French magazine, *Cahiers du Cinéma*, during the 1950s by its editor André Bazin, young film critics, and New Wave film-makers-to-be, such as Jean-Luc Godard and François Truffaut. The theory, based on the premise that the director is the "author" of a film and that each movie must be viewed in the context of the auteur's entire body of work, came to Britain through the writings of Richard Roud in *Sight and Sound*, and was introduced to the United States by its leading proponent, Andrew Sarris, in such publications as *Film Culture* and *NY Film Bulletin*. The concept fell on fertile ground, arriving in the early 1960s just as there was a burgeoning interest in the cinema. This was being fueled by revival movie houses and film societies, which showed classic films, and the growing number of "art" houses in major cities and college towns, which exhibited increasingly popular subtitled foreign-language movies.

▼ François Truffaut was the leading critical polemicist for the auteur theory. In 1960 he created *Tirez Sur Le Pianiste* (*Shoot the Piano Player*) – a modern film noir masterpiece inspired by Raoul Walsh's *High Sierra* (1941) and based on a novel by a master of pulp fiction, Davis Goodis. The casting of the pop star Charles Aznavour gave the film the feeling of being on the edge of awkwardness, which is perfect for this difficult genre. This original release *grande* for the film, with artwork by Jouineau Bourduge, is popular among collectors of New Wave posters, as is the U.S. version, which is a more stark variation.

☆ $800–1,000
☆ £525–675

☆ $500–700
☆ £325–475

▲ When the new young American and British film critics who took up the auteur theory wanted to drive the establishment mad, they would write long articles, inspired by their French counterparts, about the inner meaning and thematic substance of such great directors as Nicholas Ray and Howard Hawks. Hawks is an ideal auteur director since he consistently echoed the same themes in his work, and this 1959 film brings some of them together: men at risk and the choices they must make. The name of this one-sheet's creator has eluded all research, but it is a favorite among collectors since it utilizes cinematic perspective to capture one of the film's key moments.

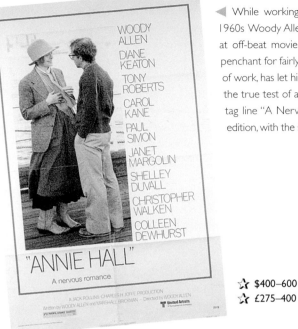

"ANNIE HALL"

A nervous romance.

While working as a stand-up comic in Greenwich Village in the early 1960s Woody Allen was a compulsive film-goer, absorbing both old and new at off-beat movie theaters, and these films lived on in his later work. His penchant for fairly low budgets and simple films, combined with a large body of work, has let his personality emerge when his work is viewed as a whole – the true test of an auteur. This 1977 original release of *Annie Hall* bears the tag line "A Nervous Romance" and is far more valuable than the second edition, with the same date and NSS number, which reads "A New Comedy."

☆ $75–100
☆ £50–75

☆ $400–600
☆ £275–400

L'INTERPRETAZIONE MUSICALE DI GIORGIO MORODER
(PREMIO OSCAR PER FLASHDANCE)
DEL CAPOLAVORO VISIONARIO DI FRITZ LANG.

Orson Welles' career as a director is cited as the ultimate vindication of the power of the auteur theory to understand the achievements of artists forced to create commercially successful movies within the constraints of the system while building an artistic profile that emerged film by film. Welles' works included outbursts of genius (*Citizen Kane*), "lost" films (*The Magnificent Ambersons*), attempts at appeasement (*Macbeth*), and totally personal works (*Mr. Arkadin*). The result is perhaps the greatest body of work produced by any one director. This Polish poster by Marszalek for a 1987 re-release of the classic *Citizen Kane* is one of the more striking visuals created worldwide.

☆ $200–300
☆ £125–200

When Fritz Lang fled Nazi Germany he sought to survive in the snakepit of Hollywood's creative refugee community. His talent was a life force; he possessed a near-brutal personality, honed razor-sharp by the frustrations of creative containment, and the inner consistency that defines an auteur. This Italian *locandino* is from the 1984 re-release of his 1926 masterpiece, *Metropolis*. The new version is fine if you turn off the soundtrack that was added by Mororder, and it did make one of the most expensive and rarest of film posters available in a theatrical release that has a powerful visual treatment of Maria the robot.

A child of the Depression Era, Clint Eastwood endured a hard scrabbled youth, and long and often frustrating years of playing bit parts and working odd jobs in Hollywood before finding success abroad, which seemed to produce in him an attitude of nonchalance towards his career. It is most fitting, therefore, that he sprung to international prominence as "The Man With No Name" in the trio of Sergio Leone spaghetti westerns, *A Fistful of Dollars*, *For a Few Dollars More,* and *The Good, The Bad and The Ugly* (filmed between 1964 and 1966). This character, and the detective Harry Callahan of the "Dirty Harry" series, were the perfect anti-hero protagonists spawned by the laconic cynicism of the mid-1960s. His attitude freed him to make a series of seemingly flawless choices of acting parts and, eventually, films to direct. His unique style and ever-growing body of work has attracted hordes of collectors, who often focus on one of the strikingly distinct genres that he effortlessly moves among, from comedy to film noir.

▼ The one-sheet for *Dirty Harry* (1971), designed by Bill Gold, set the advertising and promotional theme for the entire series. It is unlikely that this prominent use of a gun image, also featured in almost every glossy still sent to the media, could be used today, but firearms were central to the plot and in many scenes a pistol was almost a robo-cop-like extension of Eastwood's arm. The introduction of Harry Callahan was a watershed in American movies: he was the first policeman to operate outside the system, like a private eye, and audiences cheered a cop striking out at the growing tide of crime then washing over America's largest cities.

☆ $400–600
☆ £275–400

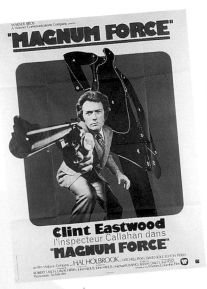

☆ $200–300
☆ £135–200

▲ *Magnum Force* was one of those rare sequels that did better than the original, though several reviewers felt that the character had been softened a bit, to appeal to more liberal instincts. But as can be seen in this French *grande*, an adaptation of Bill Gold's U.S. key art, a huge, foreshortened gun is still central to the visual theme. Hollywood has always shown a sleazy expertise at mis-directing film reviewers, creating a campaign at odds with the content of the film. They were secure in the knowledge that most critics pay little attention to film advertising. The success of this film (released 1973) was surely based on the attitude of neo-vigilantism exhibited by U.S. movie audiences at the time.

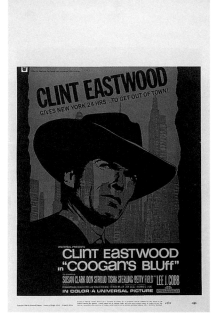

◀ This 1968 movie's title is a neat pun on a lost New York landmark (where the New York Giants baseball team once played) and Arizona lawman Coogan's oft-used deceptive ploy. The film saw the first pairing of Eastwood and director Don Siegel, a team that would create the "Dirty Harry" series. The *Coogan's Bluff* script (actually in ten different drafts) had been kicking around for years before the two men, during some stormy sessions, extracted the best elements and created an acceptable version. This almost monochromatic window card is typical of the low-key campaign for this title.

▼ The European success of Leone's first two Eastwood westerns provided him with a huge budget for the third: a three-hour epic, dramatically upgraded in technical quality, featuring hundreds of extras. Made over three years, but released in rapid succession in the U.S., the three films created the impression of one long, seamless tale of the nihilistic, nameless Eastwood character journeying through post-Civil War America. The design of this 1967 U.S. one-sheet is totally consistent with the advertising for the other films, revealing perhaps that United Artists had created one cohesive campaign for the entire series. This very "consistency" has tended to dampen the value of the posters among collectors.

▲ The fact that the illustrated poster for *A Fistful of Dollars* (1967) is a style B advance is evidence that United Artists obviously had some faith in this badly dubbed, low-budget Italian western made three years earlier and featuring an actor from a second-rate TV show. Issuing several posters before the opening of a film is a promotional program usually reserved for major releases. In fact the film became one of the top grossers of the year, catapulting Eastwood to stardom.

▼ Although this bitter-sweet Stanley Donen 1967 comedy has now found its audience – via revivals and video rentals – Hollywood didn't understand it. But there can be little doubt that the designer of this Japanese poster (20 × 28 in) was well aware of the true nature of *Two for the Road*. One can almost hear Hepburn mouthing her famous last expletive, which seems mild now but was a bit of a shocker at the time. Paper on this film is sought after, and has proven to be a popular St. Valentine's present.

As we begin to gain some perspective on the last century, the 1960s take on an increasingly pivotal role in the creation of today's behavior patterns. War, racial strife, assassinations, political turmoil, and a sexual revolution created a powerful brew that affected just about everybody – and no cultural corner escaped, including movies. Gone were the days when everyone listened to the same music, read the same bestsellers, and went to see the same films. Technology and geography combined forces to create multiple tracks of information and entertainment. There were movies for mass audiences, and specialty films imported for art houses, as well as ultra-experimental films for audiences of a few thousand. There were American independent films aimed at audiences hungry for cinema-vérité documentaries, and black films made for an audience newly sensitized to their racial identity. Hollywood, ever happy to co-opt any trend that might prove profitable, began not only to reflect the more liberal mood, but also to take full advantage of this new freedom by illustrating the changing sexual attitudes of a movie audience suddenly dominated by the younger generation.

☆ $200–300
☆ £125–200

☆ $700–900
☆ £475–600

▲ The original poster campaign for *The Graduate* (1967) was a disaster: a cartoonish mountain created by a bent leg and a minuscule drawing of Hoffman beneath it. Joseph E. Levine, the film's producer and a master showman, soon recognized the error and quickly released a poster featuring Bancroft's leg with Hoffman in the background, on which this British quad was even a slight improvement. The film is often considered the decade's most typical commercial effort; for audiences, it seemed to sum up the changes swirling around them.

Barbarella is the ultimate '60s babe — armed and dangerous, but not too liberated to perform a heated striptease during the opening credits. Based on a French comic-book character the film surpasses the form, and its vibrant colors and disjointed style put it in a class with another '60s femme fatale from the same genre, *Modesty Blaise* (1967). This 1968 British quad, designed by Robin Ray, does an even better job than the film of evoking '60s imagery. While the U.S. was entering the age of Peter Max-type drug-induced illustrations, U.K. artists were creating their own brand of L.S.D. (aka Loopy Sinuous Doodles).

 $600–800
£400–525

It is difficult to find anyone who admits to having seen this 1968 Italian film, and sadly there is no information on the poster designer, who deserves an award for so brilliantly reinventing the psychedelic experience. Only a handful of posters can have a life apart from the film for which they were created, but this is one; its use of illustrations to create a faux photomontage is a stroke of genius. Shown here is the huge Italian *quattro*, the only piece of advertising paper known to have appeared on this title.

$200–300
£125–200

$400–500
£275–325

The 1969 one-sheet for *Downhill Racer*, shown on the far right, was designed by Steve Franfurt and once made close to $900 at auction (it was rumored to have been purchased by a trendy art director for his ski chalet). The prices of all types of posters are subject to various forces: in the world of vintage travel posters those with a ski theme command a premium, and the same is true with film paper. Such diverse themes as auto racing, baseball, ballet, and images of food are attractive to collectors, and their appearance on movie posters can drive up the price of the most mundane examples. The style B one-sheet, right, offers an interesting variation using solarized imagery — a technique borrowed from the field of modern photography.

$200–300
£125–200

▼ Two new genres were created to attract audiences to the dwindling number of urban theaters: exploitation (*Truck Stop Women*, 1974, is typical) and blaxploitation. Hundreds of these were made, and the formula even percolated up into mainstream production (as in the *Terminator* and *Rambo* series). An often overlooked sub-category is the sexploitation film, and a small group of dealers and collectors specialize in these posters. Made for outside display, they are much less daring than the films.

During the 1970s demographics had a major effect on which films were made, how they were shown, and even the value of movie collectibles. The giant baby-boom generation was moving into its early marriage and child-bearing years and it was moving out of the cities in droves, creating what has come to be known as the suburbia of crabgrass America. Urban movie houses – both cinema palaces and humble neighborhood theaters – closed in the hundreds. Instead a new type of movie showcase, the multiplex, housing numerous small screening areas, appeared in the center of immense parking lots that covered paved-over farm land. This generation on the move had a new place to see movies and they wanted to see a new kind of movie. The Hollywood moguls were at a loss as to how to satisfy this changing audience, until there arose a cadre of young and exciting new talent, in the form of such directors as George Lucas, Frances Ford Coppola, Martin Scorsese, and Steven Spielberg, to fill the vacuum. As for collecting, the new theaters were configured to display only one-sheets, but the printing presses kept running and the result is a glut of never-used inserts, half-sheets, three-sheets, and lobby cards for 1970s titles.

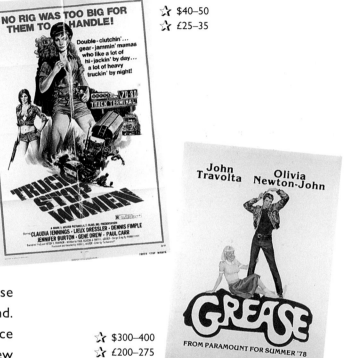

☆ $40–50
☆ £25–35

☆ $300–400
☆ £200–275

▲ In a moment of auction madness this 1978 advance poster for *Grease* once sold for $1,840. (Auction results are often far out of line with the prices quoted from dealers' catalogs and websites). While that might be excessive, it still routinely sells for several hundred dollars more than its companion, the regular release poster, which features a saccharine close-up of John Travolta and Olivia Newton-John. The higher price is attributable not only to the usual relative scarcity of advances, but also the clean graphic look of this one sheet and the manner in which it captures the retro feeling that the film, part of the 1970s nostalgia trend, was meant to project.

Arriving in the middle of the decade, *Taxi Driver* not only captures the dark underside of the 1970s, but also marks the transition from the Hollywood of cigar-chomping studio bosses to the new breed of producers/directors who had almost total control of their work. Made under the pre-'70s studio system the film would have displayed none of the brutal self-revelation portrayed by such newly emerging stars as De Niro and Foster. Guy Peellaert's one-sheet is a collector's favorite, and is an example of the long string of fine advertising graphics for films by Martin Scorsese, who, along with several other film-aficionados-turned-directors, is an avid movie-poster collector.

⭐ $100–200
⭐ £65–135

⭐ $500–600
⭐ £325–400

This one-sheet is much like *The Sting* (1973) itself: a well-crafted evocation of an earlier era. Designed by the late Richard Amsel, it could be a cover from a 1920s *Saturday Evening Post*. In the 1970s illustrators and video collagists such as Terry Gilliam often found inspiration in the graphic art of the past. Updating earlier pop culture imagery was thought very cutting-edge 30 years ago, and film posters and a handful of consumer ads were among the first manifestations of this "new" trend.

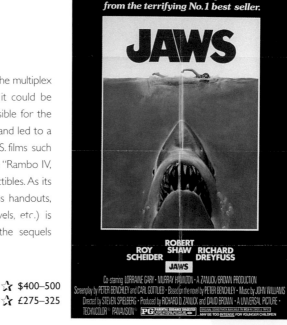

*Jaws* was the first film to demonstrate the power of the multiplex as a money machine, as its immense success meant it could be shown on several screens at once. It was also responsible for the revival of a venerated Hollywood tradition, the sequel, and led to a run on Roman numerals for the marquees of new U.S. films such as *Airport*, *Alien*, and *Halloween* (hence the industry joke "Rambo IV, audience 0."). *Jaws* also spawned its own world of collectibles. As its success was a surprise, any pre-release material (press handouts, photo-sets) or early merchandise (games, beach towels, etc.) is desirable, but the quantities of items produced as the sequels proliferated have taken a bite out of their value.

⭐ $400–500
⭐ £275–325

☆ $150–175
☆ £100–115

Things got a lot simpler in the 1980s, both for movie-goers and for collectors of memorabilia. Hollywood started filling the theaters with light comedies and action films, and at the same time it stopped producing almost all formats of movie paper except for the one-sheet. TV became the breeding ground of new movie stars as well as many of the movies themselves, and TV was where the advertising dollars to promote new films were spent. Meanwhile, cinema audiences dwindled to a dedicated tranche of the younger population, so coming-attraction trailers became powerful marketing tools, previewing highlights to a captive and responsive repeat audience. The large lobbies of the new multiplexes also became home to elaborate three-dimensional free-standing displays. The decade also saw the rise of the VCR, and the home viewing of recently shown films saw the gradual demise of the re-release. While none of these changes did much to increase the quality of the films being made, the graphic quality of movie posters gradually began to improve as a new breed of designers were given more freedom to create images that would attract the interest of an overwhelmed populace, jaded by an unending barrage of mundane advertising.

☆ $100–125
☆ £65–85

▲ The 1984 U.S. one-sheet above left is a true "teaser," since it does not include the title of the film. It is also a strong example of the time-honored Madison Avenue technique of creating a "brand image," now newly applied to movie advertising. The film itself was a super-successful combination of pop culture trends, *Saturday Night Live* type humor, and emerging technological advances in creating special effects. The regular release poster, pictured top right, is a clever evocation of the film's theme, reformatting the tag line and "no ghosts" symbol from the teaser. *Ghostbusters* spun off one sequel and, in a fitting return to its origins, a children's animated TV series.

Meet the only guy who changes his identity
more often than his underwear.

**Fletch**

CHEVY CHASE

COMING SOON TO A THEATRE NEAR YOU.

⭐ $40–50
⭐ £25–35

◄ Popular among college students, this U.S. one-sheet for Chevy Chase's 1985 comedy *Fletch* is strictly an advance, because of the "coming soon…" tag line at the bottom. But, as was increasingly the case with '80s medium-budget films, another poster was never issued, so this also became the final release version. Until the mid-'80s almost all movie posters were folded (upon printing), but as the decade wore on exhibition levels disappeared and they were rolled and sent directly to the one location playing the film. The example pictured was rolled, and brings a higher price than folded versions from this transition period.

⭐ $200–300
⭐ £135–200

They've been laughed at, picked on and put down.
But now it's time for the odd to get even!

**REVENGE OF THE NERDS**

• Their time has come! •

REVENGE OF THE NERDS

⭐ $25–30
⭐ £15–20

*IT'S ONE HUNDRED AND SIX MILES TO GO. WE GOT A FULL TANK O' GAS, HALF A PACK OF CIGARETTES, IT'S DARK, AND WE'RE WEARING SUNGLASSES!*

*HIT IT.*

The Blues Brothers
COMING SOON

The show that really hits the road.

JOHN BELUSHI DAN AYKROYD

**The Blues Brothers**
The most devastating team since
nitro and glycerine.

OUCH!

⭐ $200–300
⭐ £135–200

▲ Steven Chorney, designer of this 1984 one-sheet for *Revenge of the Nerds*, was a prolific illustrator whose work could serve as a template for 1980s poster art. He created posters for dozens of films, including *Ice Pirates*, *Ladyhawke*, *Oxford Blues*, and *Ordinary People*. But he was no stranger to failure, having been responsible for the key art for *Ishtar*, one of cinema's magnificent disasters, nor to low-end comedies, having worked on *Caddyshack II* and *Ernest Goes to Jail*, as well as *Nerds*.

▲ Pictured are the regular-release quad for *The Blues Brothers* (1980) and an advance poster, a style seldom used in the U.K, where even A and B styles are scarce. By the early '80s Hollywood was picking up marketing ideas from consumer corporations, and with the changes in distribution and exhibition brought on by the new movie houses, choices had to be made as to what to be printed for each film. If a studio had confidence in a title, as in this case, it would budget more for ancillary posters, displays, and promotional giveaways.

# James Bond

The James Bond series of films is a collector's paradise, consisting of a completely enclosed universe that expands on a regular, if not frequent, basis. It is filled with anomalies, variations, errors, and all the slight inconsistencies that allow aficionados to become experts. It also projects the illusion of attainability, beckoning with the notion that one day it might be possible to assemble a complete collection of posters for each of the films. However, this is a cruel mirage since every book published and auction held reveals more and more previously unknown styles, sub-sets, re-issues, re-strikes, and a bewildering array of small differences in size and color. It seems that the very type of person who is attracted to the films is also just that type of collector who revels in all this minutiae. The images on these pages are mainly one-sheets, but the Bond films, especially the early ones, were issued when all of the major formats were being produced, and several new sizes were created solely to promote the 007 phenomenon. Chief among these is the super-large poster designed for use in transit systems and bus shelters.

▼ When it comes to Bond memorabilia, there are two distinct price categories: one for the everyday movie paper collectors and another for Bond collectors, who are more interested in the massive number of 007 toys, props, and spin-offs (see p.132). The latter's needs are often sated in huge sales at major auction houses, such as Christie's, London — the catalogs (now collectors' items themselves) filled with all the stuff that 007 dreams are made of. Interspersed among the treasures is a selection of posters that sell way above the usual market price, skewing the value structure. This *Dr. No* poster by David Chasman is the original 1962 release U.S. one-sheet, a basic building block for a personal Bond poster archive.

☆ $1,600–1,800
☆ £1,075–1,200

☆ $700–1,000
☆ £475–675

▲ The style A U.S. release one-sheet for *From Russia With Love* (1963), above right, was also designed by Chasman. Although the look of the posters didn't improve with the second film, the quality of the movie did: this is considered the best of the Bonds. Sean Connery's acting career was on a downward spiral when he was picked to play Bond, for which he was perfect. As the series unfolded, a parasitical synergy between Connery and the creative team led to ever-better performances, and scenes molded to suit his personality. All the paper on this film shares the same dull look, which accounts for the lower prices this title usually fetches.

☆ $900–1,200
☆ £600–800

☆ $2,500–3,000
☆ £1,675–2,000

☆ $1,200–1,500
☆ £800–1,000

▲ By the time *Goldfinger* was released in 1964 United Artists knew this was more than a series, it was a franchise, and it poured out promotional material. These are the most popular Bond posters and, despite the huge quantity available, they still attract strong prices. The British quad by John Robert Brown is a style B – style A shows the same image of Connery and Blackman but inside a golden body instead of a hand. The one- and three-sheets by Chasman come much closer to capturing the mood of the film, which established the tone for the rest of the series: cryptic one-liners, double entendres, plus action that no longer paid even lip service to reality.

☆ $900–1,200
☆ £600–800

☆ $300–400
☆ £200–275

▲ In 1981 U.A. did no one a favor by faithfully reproducing the first four Bond one-sheets to promote a re-release package. The posters were sent out rolled (but unscrupulous dealers may neatly fold them), printed on slick paper (which may be covered up if they are linen-mounted). Happily, all have minor differences from the originals. In this one-sheet by Frank McCarthy and Robert McGinnis, Connery's jetpack is extended right through the top margin, while in the reproduction it is truncated at the edge line.

▶ George Lazenby was Connery's heir, but the change proved unpopular and this 1969 film did poorly. The one-sheet, designed by Frank McCarthy, is one of the better Bond images but lacks appeal, perhaps because of its association with the film. Connery returned in 1971 with *Diamonds Are Forever* and the hiatus was filled by the only Ian Fleming title that escaped U.A., *Casino Royale*. The psychedelic look of that campaign has propelled paper from *Royale* to the higher end of the Bond spectrum, with the rare and striking door panels featuring each of the major characters often fetching auction prices in the thousands.

The date May 25, 1977, marks not only the U.S. opening of *Star Wars* but also the beginning of modern movie-poster collecting. Until that time only an esoteric clique of collectors had sought out and accumulated original film paper, but with the huge success and impact of what was to become the first science-fiction mega-movie, anything associated with the film was an immediate collectible. Since only a handful of the many ancillary items had yet appeared, attention focused on the posters. One of the *Star Wars* myths holds that Twentieth Century-Fox had little faith in the film and did almost nothing to promote it. This is belied by the fact that four special advance posters were made before the film opened, and that the regular-release promotional material was issued in a full complement of sizes and formats, including a standee and a banner-treatment normally reserved for an "A" release. What was not unusual, but which had a distinct bearing on collecting memorabilia related to the *Star Wars* phenomenon, was that the film opened in less than 100 theaters nationwide (unlike the thousands that are used today). The subsequent paucity of original items and the convergence of scarcity and rarity created a perfect storm of frenzied collecting.

▼ Made to be sold at the 1976 World Science-Fiction Convention in Kansas City, this 20 x 29 in (51 x 74 cm) poster is the first *Star Wars* image. It was designed by the artist Harold Chaykin, and the majority of surviving examples are signed by him. Mark Hamil, one of the film's stars, was also present at the convention and autographed many of the posters. The design bears no relation to later *Star Wars* artwork, suggesting a hasty conception by Fox to publicize their forthcoming top release at a relevant major event. They badly underestimated how many would attend, as only a thousand or so posters were printed.

☆ $2,000–3,000
☆ £1,325–2,000

☆ $400–500
☆ £275–325

▲ This 1977 one-sheet was designed by Tom Jung and sets the tone for the entire opening campaign. It came in a wide range of sizes, including one sheet, insert, half-sheet, 30 x 40, and 40 x 60, and is the basis of *Star Wars* poster collecting. In order to get the film in as many theaters as possible, extra posters and promotional material was printed. There are four editions of the style A, all issued while the film was in its first release. One has a hairline crack just below Luke Skywalker's belt; although an original, it has become known as a faux-reproduction and its collectible viability has been tainted.

▶ It is a galactic myth that the only *Star Wars* image to hang in director George Lucas' home is the original artwork for this style "D" poster. Created by Drew Struzan and Charles White III, it is known as The Circus Poster because it harks back to the early days of sideshow stone lithographs. It was issued during the first year of the film's release to refresh the campaign; when it was reprinted for the re-release of 1992 the letter D marker at the bottom of the poster had no quote marks, distinguishing it from the original. The poster's rich complexity makes fuzzy reproductions easy to spot.

☆ $400–500
☆ £275–325

☆ $2,500–3,000
☆ £1,675–2,000

☆ $3,000–3,500
☆ £2,000–2,325

▲ To mark the 1978 anniversary of the opening of *Star Wars* Fox issued this poster, which was designed by Tony Seiniger and Associates with photography by Weldon Anderson. It exists only as a one sheet and, with the inclusion of the Kenner toy figures, has become a great example of a cross-collectible as it is sought after by both poster and toy collectors. The poster was sent to all theaters that were still playing the film after a year, which was about 500 sites. It is estimated that less than a thousand were printed and most of those found on the market today originate from the small bakery in Brooklyn that created the cake in the photo. Fox sent them a couple of rolls of posters as a gift; a New York dealer bought the entire batch and has been feeding them into the market ever since.

▶ It was planned that a series of *Star Wars* concerts would be held in major cities across the USA during the 1978–79 film season and this poster, designed by Suzy Rice-Lane with an illustration by John Alvin, was to be used at each event. But after the first and only concert, held at the Hollywood Bowl in Los Angeles on November 20, 1978, the remainder of the tour was canceled. As a result this poster, which measures 24½ x 37 in, was sold on that night alone and it has become the most desirable of the non-movie-theater *Star Wars* posters, as only a handful exist in the marketplace.

▲ This style A poster for *The Empire Strikes Back*, issued for the initial release in 1981 with art by Roger Kastel, was pulled because of objections by Billy Dee Williams that his name had been omitted from the acting credits. Dubbed "the Gone with the Wind poster" because of the lovers' pose, which harks back to Roger Soubie's classic imagery for that film's post-World War II campaign, it was issued in a full range of formats. The U.S. release, which has no NSS number, is of equal value to the international version. The poster shown is framed, which is usually a red flag, although this one-sheet was vetted and sold at Skinner's, Boston. Frames can hide defects and dreaded dry-mounting, which just about ruins the value of a poster.

▲ George Lucas had no real say in the early promotion of the 1977 release of *Star Wars* (as opposed to the total control he now exercises over every aspect of the films) and Twentieth Century-Fox was so overwhelmed by the film's U.S. success that it left its European offices to their own devices when promoting the film. Nowhere is this more obvious than with the Italian *due Guerre Stellari*. Executed as a cartoon by the artist Papuzza, it was quickly withdrawn and only seems to exist in the large format. It was replaced by the standard U.S. Tom Jung art, shown above, except that Darth Vader looms with much greater prominence than in any of the other versions.

▶ Illustrated is the one-sheet for the third film in the trilogy, *Return Of The Jedi* (1983), designed by Paykos Phior from an illustration by Tim Reamer. It was to be the advance poster, but time constraints led it to be used as the style A poster for the initial release. (The true advance was the pair of *Revenge of the Jedi* posters – the rare one without a date and the more common dated one, neither of which received extensive use because of the name change.) Style A did not last long in theaters and was soon replaced by style B, which features Luke swinging a LightSaber over the heads of all the characters. A reproduction of style A exists but, as with most illicit copies, the printing is blurry and muddy.

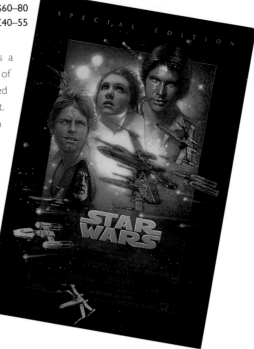

▶ In 1997, to mark the 20th anniversary of its release (and as a promotional run-up to *Episode 1*), Lucas presented a Special Edition of the first three *Star Wars* films, re-formatted, digitally enhanced with added scenes, and free popcorn for every "Wookie" that bought a ticket. There were four posters, one master for the entire re-presentation and one for each film. They were all issued both single- and double-sided, which makes 16 posters in all. The revival was so popular that the play dates of the third film had to be pushed back: the initial Jedi poster states March 7 but another was issued, single- and double-sided, with a corrected date of March 14. The entire set of posters was designed by Drew Struzen and they all sell within the price guide given for the one illustrated right.

◀ The frenzy that surrounded the appearance of the first one-sheet for the 1999 release of *Episode 1: The Phantom Menace* serves as a cautionary tale for poster collectors. At one point copies of this poster were trading for over $1,000. While Lucas released single-sided versions through the *Star Wars* fan club, only double-sided posters were sent to theaters, and then with strict orders not to let them be sold. No replacement for "damaged" posters would be sent and any flagrant attempts to sell them for a profit would strike the theater from the film's play list. This was stated in a letter from Lucas Film to each venue and it caused a market squeeze that lasted until the film had completed its run. Values have now returned to some sensible level: the single-sided poster sells for about $75 and the impressive 24 x 81in banner in the $500 range.

Illustrators

While traditionally the collecting of movie paper has been driven by films and their stars, a third major area has opened up with the increased interest in the designer of film posters and advertising campaigns. A dearth of information existed about this army of what was thought to be anonymous commercial illustrators, until research slowly revealed that not only studio hacks, but some quite famous names were involved in creating the displays that covered the front of movie theaters for the last hundred years. Such self-promoters as Saul Bass were well known, but emerging information that Norman Rockwell, J.C. Leyendecker, James Montgomery Flagg, and Al Hirschfeld had also worked in the field led to further research about such lesser-known artists as Bill Gold (*Casablanca*) and Reynold Brown (*Creature from the Black Lagoon*). While parallels can be drawn with the heightened interest in the golden age of American illustration, which has led to some major sales, this is one area of movie collectibles that has not proven immensely popular. Original artwork for film posters does show up at auction but, with a few notable exceptions, collectors eschew it in favor of the printed version.

☆ $30–40
☆ £20–25

☆ $40–50
☆ £25–35

▲ The late Bob Peak was a prolific and masterful illustrator and his campaign for *My Fair Lady* is illustrated here by the cover of the souvenir book, sold in large theaters during the initial run of the film and representative of the key art. Peak's flower-filled design is a reflection of the Pop Art trends that were emerging when the film opened in 1964. The program cover for *Paint Your Wagon* (1969) represents Pop Art come full circle: an artistic movement, inspired by commercial imagery, now recycled to sell a movie. The artwork is by the master of this trickery, Peter Max, but he did not do the full campaign, only this and a set of six limited-edition posters.

◄ Even the most mediocre careers can have a defining moment, and Jack Davis, a cartoonist illustrator whose work includes the posters for *The Long Goodbye*, *One More Time*, and *Viva Max*, was obviously challenged to a peak of creativity by Stanley Kramer's frantic comedy, *It's A Mad, Mad, Mad, Mad World*. Seldom does a key campaign image show exactly what a film is about, but Davis' illustration is the movie in a shell of nutcases! The landscape format of this 1964 U.K. quad was ideal for adapting the original U.S. artwork, which, constrained by the vertical one-sheet, was now able to burst out in full force and capture the film's central device – a money-driven madcap chase.

☆ $300–400
☆ £200–275

▼ The Academy Cinema in London introduced most of the foreign classics to British audiences, and from the 1940s to 1970s many of their posters were created by Peter Strausfield. Printing from lino-blocks, as on this 1951 double-crown for *Murder In The Cathedral*, he produced over 300 posters for such movies as *The Rules of the Game* and *The Seventh Seal*. Whether in this smaller format or more typical larger quads, his work is distinctive and recognizable. Only 100–300 copies of this poster were made but, though by a noted artist, they fail to reach high values as collectors focus on the standard imagery.

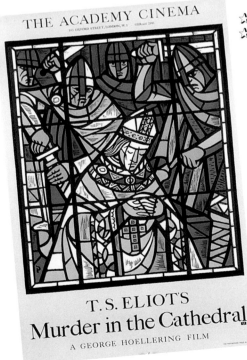

☆ $200–300
☆ £125–200

☆ $800–1,000
☆ £525–675

▲ Illustrator Tomi Ungerer designed only one other movie poster aside from *Dr. Strangelove* – the one-sheet for *Monterey Pop* – but his imagery for Stanley Kubrick's 1964 Cold War comedy appeared on just about every advertising format around the world and is still used to this day when the film is revived or re-released. One of a group of New York-based highbrow cartoonists in the 1960s, along with such talents as Edward Gorey and Saul Steinberg, Ungerer is better-known as a book illustrator. While the image on this three-sheet is his artwork, the poster itself was laid out by designer Pablo Ferro.

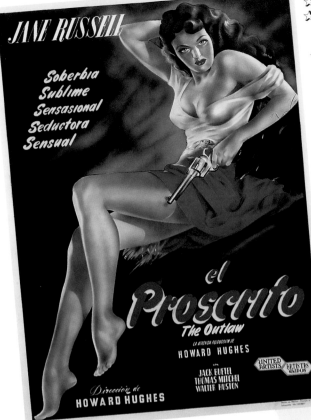

☆ $2,000–3,000
☆ £1,325–2,000

◀ *The Outlaw* was completed in 1943 but producer Howard Hughes spent three years battling censors before the movie was given a general release. Most of the controversy was over the revealing imagery of Jane Russell, as presented in several, now famous, black-and-white stills and this daring movie poster. While Hughes made several concessions to secure the U.S. release, the Mexican one-sheet illustrated here seems to have escaped unscathed and is close to designer Zoe Mozart's original concept. Mozart studied with Maxfield Parrish and N.C. Wyeth in her youth and, during the 1930s, become one of the few female artists to draw pin-ups. She designed hundreds of magazine covers, calendars, and other movie posters, chief among them Carole Lombard's 1937 comedy, *True Confession*.

▶ Master of the air brush, and the most prolific of pin-up artists, Alberto Vargas (aka Varga) would take occasional breaks from crafting calendars, magazine layouts, and even arcade cards, to design a movie poster. During the '30s and '40s a series of films was released with advertising artwork portraying his undulating female imagery. A single poster from this 20-year span stands out – this one sheet for *Moon Over Miami*, in which all the artist's skills were matched with perhaps his greatest model, Betty Grable. The resultant poster has been as elusive as it is compelling, and very few examples come on the market. While many other films from 1941 are represented by copious examples of paper, it can only be assumed that this striking image languished in the rooms of projectionists and teenage ushers, lost forever to the traditional trove of collectible movie paper.

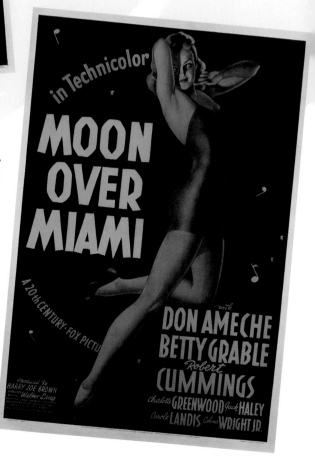

☆ $5,000–6,000
☆ £3,325–4,000

This lobby card from the 1933 melodrama *Frisco Jenny* is an excellent example of the decorated border format so popular in the 1920s and '30s. This particular illustration is uncredited, but it is in the style of Earl Moran and some have attributed it to Vargas, or it could be just a talented studio illustrator working in the popular style. There are a handful of collectors who seek out elaborate border cards such as this, where the film image is overwhelmed by the motif element. While most borders are related to the content of the movie, some are more abstract – Art Deco ones have an explosion of geometric shapes in vibrant colors.

★ $60–80
★ £40–55

★ $100–200
★ £65–125

Few artists define an age so completely as John Held Jr. does the "Roaring Twenties." His simple images of flappers and college guys in raccoon coats, often in a woodblock medium, shaped and recorded the images of a generation. As well as cartoons and theater sets, he created a small number of movie posters, including this window card for *So This Is College* (1929). Its trading history is enlightening: in 1991, at the start of the movie-poster boom, a one-sheet sold at auction for $2,475. Three years later another card was offered at $2,500 and finally sold in 1999 for $115, and in 2000 a one-sheet sold for just $88.

The famed American illustrator James Montgomery Flagg (noted for the "Uncle Sam Wants You" World War I image) did a handful of movie-poster designs, but this one-sheet for *Lost Horizon* (1937) almost wasn't one of them. Columbia felt that a classy film needed a highbrow campaign so they hired a big-name artist to execute the advertising art. But the studio was not pleased with Flagg's work and, gathering by the results, just about everyone in the promotion department had an attempt at revising it. Often mis-identified as style D, the one-sheet illustrated is actually style C (styles A and B seem never to have existed.) Flagg's artwork was used in other formats, such as the half-sheet, and most command high prices.

★ $5,000–6,000
★ £3,325–4,000

JOHN WAYNE · KIRK DOUGLAS
PATRICIA NEAL · TOM TRYON · PAULA PRENTISS
BRANDON de WILDE · JILL HAWORTH
DANA ANDREWS & HENRY FONDA

IN HARM'S WAY
AN OTTO PREMINGER FILM

CO-STARRING
STANLEY HOLLOWAY · BURGESS MEREDITH · FRANCHOT TONE · PATRICK O'NEAL · CARROLL O'CONNOR
SLIM PICKENS · JAMES MITCHUM · GEORGE KENNEDY · BRUCE CABOT · BARBARA BOUCHET
SCREENPLAY BY WENDELL MAYES · BASED ON THE NOVEL BY JAMES BASSETT · MUSIC BY JERRY GOLDSMITH · PRODUCTION DESIGNED BY
LYLE WHEELER · PHOTOGRAPHED IN PANAVISION® BY LOYAL GRIGGS · A PARAMOUNT RELEASE · PRODUCED AND DIRECTED BY OTTO PREMINGER

SAINT JOAN

▲ ▶ The poster-design career of Saul Bass is the most oft-cited reference for this area of movie-paper collecting. He first attracted attention for his work on the opening credits of such films as *Walk on the Wild Side* and *West Side Story*, creating an entire minifilm before the main feature began. He also became known for his film-advertising work, and the one-sheets pictured, *In Harm's Way* (1965) and *Saint Joan* (1957), illustrate not only his ability to capture the mood of a film while creating a striking and commercial ad campaign, but also the affordability of many of his designs. Images such as those for *Vertigo* and *Bonjour Tristesse* sell for thousands, but other films such as *The Cardinal* and *Bunny Lake is Missing*, are still plentiful and fairly reasonably priced.

Frank Frazetta started his career as a comic-book illustrator in the mid-1940s, worked with famed cartoonist Al Capp in the '50s, and became a much sought-after book-cover designer in the early '60s. In 1965 he turned to serious painting, focusing on increasingly popular fantasy subjects, and he was soon once again creating commercial campaigns for not only paperbacks and off-beat magazines but a series of Hollywood movies. This one-sheet for *The Gauntlet* (1977) is classic Frazetta, and his work was so popular by this time that the studio issued a promotional version of this poster without text that sells for close to three times the value. Other examples of his work are *Conan The Barbarian* and *What's New Pussycat*.

 $300–400
£200–275

$50–75
£35–50

$60–80
£40–55

 Robert Peak created this half-sheet and the entire ad campaign for the first *Star Trek* film in 1979. He also worked on several later editions of the saga but the initial designs set the overall tone for the entire series. This is typical of Peak's work – his imagery goes directly to the core of a film and influences its entire career. When the re-edited *Apocalypse Now* was released in 2001 Peak's original poster art was the obvious choice, and though he designed the key art only for the first *Superman*, all later versions refer to his visual themes.

Reynold Brown is an example of a prolific and unsung commercial illustrator whose work was rescued from obscurity by dedicated collectors and dealers. Starting in the early 1950s with the poster for *The World in his Arms*, he worked on over 250 films in all formats, from window cards to billboards. This three-sheet from 1960's *The Alamo* is typical of his highly detailed work that creates an almost unreal atmosphere – perhaps why some of his best work was in sci-fi and fantasy. His *Creature from the Black Lagoon* and *The Time Machine* posters are auction favorites.

Meet Philip Marlowe. The toughest private eye who ever wore a trench coat, slapped a dame and split his knuckles on a jawbone.

☆ $50–75
☆ £35–50

▲ ▼ Richard Amsel began his 17-year career as a commercial designer in true Hollywood style: as a student he won a contest, sponsored by Twentieth Century-Fox, to create the campaign for *Hello Dolly* (1968). The 50-plus movie-poster images and two-dozen TV-guide covers that followed lifted him to the top rank of entertainment illustrators. This 1978 one-sheet for *The Big Sleep* is typical of his technical skill, brought to bear on the retro theme of a film noir tour-de-force. The 1977 *Julia* one-sheet displays his ability at contemporary imagery, while projecting the aura of duplicity that is the film's sub-text. His posters are immediately recognizable as Amsels, but his unique style never overpowered the primary aim to intrigue and to entice viewers to the movies.

☆ $40–50
☆ £25–35

☆ $300–400
☆ £200–265

▶ Martin Scorsese's *Raging Bull* (1980) has been showered with awards and is often voted one of the best films of the last three decades. Just as well regarded is the poster of Robert De Niro as Jake La Motta, and the regular-release one-sheet illustrated is part of a trio that includes the advance and the international style, all of which are consistent favorites at film memorabilia auctions. The three posters vary in layout but share the same striking image of De Niro, as created by designer Kunio Hagio – a meticulous artist, who has done just a handful of movie campaigns. The original artwork for *Raging Bull* was offered at Christie's L.A. in a large sale of source material for film posters. Overcoming the usual reticence among collectors to such items, the oil-on-gessoed-masonite was one of few pieces to sell, and exceeded its guide price of $30,000 (£20,000).

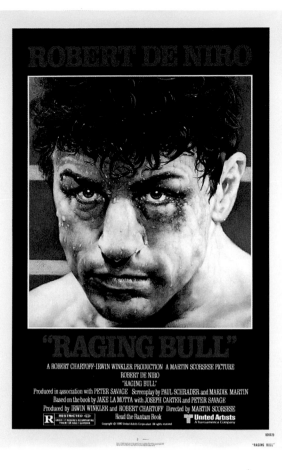

◀ Peruvian-born illustrator Boris Vallejo came to the USA in 1964 unable to speak English and with just $80 in his pocket. Starting out as a designer of Christmas cards, and moving on to advertising work, he soon became one of the top comic-book artists, specializing in images of terrifying monsters, bizarre winged creatures and heroes replete with bulging muscles. His proto-fantasy bias was prominently at play in selecting him to create the campaign for the *National Lampoon Vacation* series, and it is obvious he wasn't above poking a bit of fun at the better-known aspects of his work. This 1985 one-sheet for the second film is a satire on a take-off, since the first artwork, from 1983, has the characters in the same pose but with slightly different props and background. His other well-known posters include *Winged Serpent* and *Hercules* (both 1983).

☆ $60–80
☆ £40–55

# Re-releases

In the early days of cinema films never went out of release, but just played constantly to a new and ever-growing audience. However, after the first full-length feature and the start of the star system, whereby actors were bound by contract to the studios, the re-issuing of older films became a viable marketing ploy and recycled two-reeler comedy shorts, especially Charlie Chaplin ones, became a staple of the industry. The marketing material is now popular with collectors. After the majors joined the National Screen Scheme in the late 1930s, a re-release was usually indicated by a letter R in front of the NSS number (in the lower-right corner of many posters). The next two digits are the year of the re-release, followed by the stock number. The image might be the same as the original, but often it was printed in garish duotones or had dropped several colors. Sometimes a new graphic was created altogether, especially if several years had passed since the original release. By the 1930s most of the majors had set up a separate distribution arm just to handle re-releases, and created such names as Realart (Universal) and Masterpiece Productions (United Artists), with no other indication that the film was on another go-around.

☆ $400–600
☆ £275–400

▲ Not all re-release posters are less valuable than the originals, and the posters for *The Hustler* are the oft-cited textbook example. Twentieth Century-Fox doubted the appeal of a movie about pool players, so their initial campaign, as seen in the 1961 three-sheet on the right, played it as a torrid romance. After its huge success, the pool theme was boldly featured for its 1964 re-issue, as shown in this one-sheet. Fox actually took this imagery from the *grande*, designed by Jean Mascii for the film's initial French release. *The Hustler* is one of those "cross interest" posters, with price pressure also being exerted by an avid group of pool ephemera collectors.

▶ Stanley Kubrick was noted for micro-managing every aspect of the release of his films, from poster imagery right down to the size of the newspaper ads, and this is what makes the 1982 re-release one-sheet such an anomaly. How a poster that captures the horror of the famed re-training sequence and the hoodlum gang violence survived for this one brief moment is a mystery, albeit a graphically pleasing one. The initial campaign, and all the re-issues after this one, features the Philip Castle design: a grinning image of Alex inside a triangle – with or without a knife, depending on the country of release.

▲ *La Dolce Vita*, the first Italian film to become an international success, played in first-run theaters, not just in the specialty houses usually reserved for foreign films. It had rolling premieres around the world for the first few years after its release in 1960, for which a plethora of advertising material was produced. There are no bargains to be had when buying original release material and even the posters from other countries issued close to 1960 are quite expensive. But the film has had several major re-releases and this 1972 French *grande* is a good alternative. Its Art Nouveau look is much influenced by the late '60s/early '70s San Francisco psychedelic style.

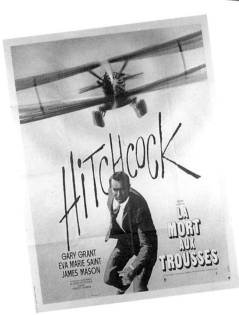

▲ Saul Bass' 1959 poster for the original release of *North By Northwest* was one of his lesser efforts, and did little to capture the mood of one of Hitchcock's most suspenseful films. That certainly can't be said of Landi's *grande* for the 1991 re-release in France. Posters issued a few years after a movie's opening have this advantage, as by this time it has become clear which scene or theme has captured the audience's imagination. There is also a rare re-issue one-sheet showing the famed Mount Rushmore sequence.

☆ $35–40
☆ £23–27

◀ Several years ago The American Film Institute compiled a list of the 100 funniest films ever made, with *Some Like It Hot* (1959) at the top spot. Around the same time The British Film Institute initiated a series of re-releases of selected film classics. Using brand new prints and a specially created poster, the first movie to be selected was this Billy Wilder comedy, starring Tony Curtis, Jack Lemmon, and Marilyn Monroe. Some of the films in the series had limited showings at the National Film Theatre in London and a few other chosen venues, while others with corporate backing were released nationally. The quad created for each film was a clever re-working of the original one-sheet.

☆ $40–45
☆ £27–30

▲ The BFI series of re-issue posters were printed in limited numbers and were available, on a restricted basis, for authorized re-sale since, like all theatrical film posters, they were not created for commercial purposes. This was strictly enforced, especially in the London area, but, as always, a few slipped through and appeared on the open market. The quad for *Singin' In The Rain* (R2000) has about doubled in price since it first appeared, and now that collectors are vying to assemble a complete set of the BFI revival series, the few copies available will become more difficult to obtain. The graphic design on this poster is a rehash of the 1952 original but is more dynamic through its elimination of wasted white space.

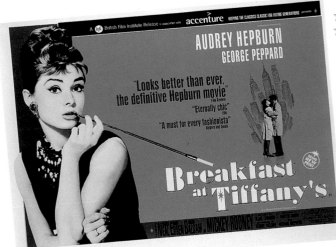

$150–200
£100–125

◀ Of the posters created so far for this series *Breakfast At Tiffany's* was the most highly anticipated, and became an instant rarity. The power of the advertising imagery was carried over from the 1961 original release and, as with all the re-issues, the designer relied heavily on the key art, gleaned from early pressbooks. The result is a pastiche of the first campaign, with a late '90s twist evident in the treated photo of Hepburn (as opposed to the illustrated look of the original) and the use of a blue and brown color scheme. Within a short time this quad will evoke the millennium in the same way that the earlier one-sheet recalls the graphic look of the early 1960s.

$40–50
£27–35

▶ The prominent mention of "3-D" on this re-release quad for *Kiss Me Kate* is, along with its limited availability, a strong factor in forcing up the value. Exhibiting films in 3-D was an attempt by Hollywood in the early 1950s to fight back the rising tide of TV viewing. Fervent collectors of 3-D memorabilia have a small market, as most 3-D films received only limited showings. After playing the big downtown theaters the films were released "flat", which is why many posters have the references to 3-D blacked out, thus decreasing their value.

$35–40
£23–27

◀ Cross pressures, this time from collectors of blaxploitation material, will also affect the value of this re-issue quad for 1971's *Shaft*. The original release of this film, directed by noted photographer Gordon Parks and starring Richard Roundtree, was early in the cycle of black-themed action films. Of the posters issued to date for this BFI series, *Shaft* is the best adaptation of the graphics from the original portrait one-sheet to the landscape dimensions of this UK quad. The unnamed designer utilized the cinematic aspect of the British poster format by creating a much tighter image, and by moving up the title, the blazing gun has been obscured – a necessary visual edit in these more sensitive times.

Ever on the prowl to find new ways of pushing their product, the major movie companies have latched on to just about every development and trend in display over the last 100 or so years, adopting, discarding, and then rediscovering a wide range of formats as they invent and reinvent the wheel of promotion. Movie posters were heir to the printing technology used to advertise the great outdoor shows of the late 19th century, and as stone lithography gave way to metal-plate printing, and then to high-speed presses that could create large quantities of full-color paper, the film industry rode the wave of change. Such innovations as coated stocks, double-sided printing, and UV-sensitive inks were met with enthusiasm, and no expense was spared to spread the word about a film. New techniques such as printing on mylar and holographic lenticulars also had brief periods of popularity, but have faded from use as the majors rely more and more on the simple one-sheet and elaborate lobby displays. This, combined with use of TV advertising time, carefully crafted coming-attraction trailers, and interviews via satellite with the films' stars, are the major methods of currently attracting audiences. The newest innovation is a digital poster, with images and text that can be changed by a click of the mouse.

▼ This 1910 three-sheet for *Cowboy Millionaire* was relined (taken off its original backing and put onto duck canvas for restoration) when presented at a New York auction several years ago. Printed in England, it was most likely placed on cloth soon after coming off the press, since it was designed to be hung outside the myriad venues used to show films, such as tents, halls, and schools, before the first feature film, *The Birth of A Nation* (1912), created a demand for purpose-built cinemas. *Cowboy Millionaire* was produced by William Selig, a pioneer showman who set up the first studio in Hollywood.

☆ $1,000–2,000
☆ £675–1,325

☆ $2,500–3,000
☆ £1,675–2,000

▲ Printed on silver mylar paper (which has a chrome finish) this one-sheet, designed by advertising agency Doyle, Dane, and Bernbach, was the first *Star Wars* advance and an early example of the printing method. It was shipped to theaters in a flat box since rolling it caused delamination – a separation of the printed elements from the surface. It was first seen in lobbies during the Christmas season of 1976, five months before the opening. Only a small number exist in any tradeable condition and, since they are impossible to restore, this quantity will remain fixed or may decrease if the posters become vulnerable to the delamination process.

☆ $4,000–5,000
☆ £2,675–3,325

☆ $100–200
☆ £65–125

▶ It was 1993 before Hollywood again used the lenticular to promote a film and then two appeared at once: *Meteor Man* and *Nightmare Before Christmas*. The quality of a lenticular is determined by the number of layers in the "sandwich" – each layer creating more depth but also increasing the cost. *The Frighteners* (1998), shown right, is of medium quality, while *Nightmare Before Christmas* is superior and, as a film with a cult following, routinely fetches over $1,500.

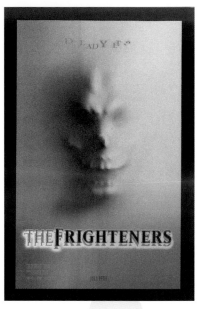

▲ The lenticular poster is a plastic sandwich that creates a holographic 3-D image when light is poured through it. Earlier, mechanical lenticulars had angled slats to create a similar effect, but this new technique was first used in film promotion for Stanley Kubrick's *2001* (1968). Shown is the large-format version (23 × 33 in), produced in the "space wheel" style, with less than 20 known to exist. Two smaller (11 × 14-in) lenticulars were made for the initial Cinerama release, one featuring the space wheel, the other showing the astronauts on the moon's surface. These both sell for around $1,500 (£1,000).

☆ $600–800
☆ £400–525

◀ Credited with being among the earliest mylar movie posters, this advance one-sheet for *Rollerball* appeared shortly before the film opened in the summer of 1975. The regular-format posters for the film routinely sell in the $60 to $80 range, and though only one of these laminated styles has so far been discovered, it has yet to sell for much more than ten times that value. This is an example of the difference between scarcity and rarity: an object must be desirable as well as unobtainable. Other notable mylars include *Nashville* (1975), *Black Sunday* (1977), Mick Jagger's *Freejack* (1992) and the more recent *Charlie's Angels* (2000). The technique is often used for anniversary posters, as with the 1987 re-release of *Snow White* and several re-issues of the *Star Wars* saga.

▼ While Twentieth Century-Fox firmly believed in the box-office potential of *Star Wars* and backed it with a complete promotion campaign, the same cannot be said of the nation's theater owners if their reluctance to purchase this banner is any indication. Perhaps it was the then stiff $35 price that deterred them but, whatever the reason, only a handful were shipped and the balance were reportedly discarded. Made of nylon and measuring 81 in long and 2 ft high, only three examples are known to exist.

☆ $3,000–4,000
☆ £2,000–2,675

# Other Memorabilia

*If* The Mummy *poster is the apex of movie-paper collecting, Dorothy's ruby slippers from* The Wizard of Oz *represent the ultimate collectible from cinema memorabilia's nether world of props, autographs, and all the ephemera and detritus of film production and promotion. It is ironic that two of the most beloved films,* It's A Wonderful Life *and* The Wizard of Oz, *were both unsuccessful initially and achieved their ultimate fame through repeated showings on TV – the technological advance that was supposedly the death knell of movies. Any item associated with these films takes on iconic stature, and the slippers illustrated sold at Christie's, New York, in May 2000 for $666,000. Seven pairs were made for use in the 1939 film and four are known to exist, their movements and current ownership tracked with the intensity and devotion usually reserved for a religious relic – a reverence perfectly in keeping with the new obsession for collecting Hollywood's past.*

# Press Kits and Pressbooks

Press kits and pressbooks are two of the more easily confused movie-paper terms. They were both created by the studio publicity department, but for quite different purposes. The press kit, developed in the 1970s, is a package, usually in a folder with some aspect of the key art on the cover, containing a group of stills (see pp.112–113) and sometimes slides, plus printed material presenting the official credits, a synopsis, biographies of the stars and chief crew, and a production background story. The press kit is sent to film critics, entertainment editors, and others in the media. The pressbook is a much older marketing tool that was sent to movie-theater owners in the days when films played in a variety of venues (see p.102.) It contained sample ads, suggestions on how to promote the film, product tie-ins and, most important to collectors, illustrations of the various posters that could be ordered from the National Screen Service (see p.17) or from the film studio direct.

**PRESSBOOK**

☆ $15–20
☆ £10–14

▲ This 1975 pressbook for the original release of *Dog Day Afternoon* illustrates the value of these pieces of commercial ephemera to the collector. The back page shows the insert, the standard one-sheet (on the left), a three-sheet (bottom right and mis-named as a one-sheet) and the half-sheet, also referred to as a "display." The text refers to other items that could be ordered: eight color 8 × 10s (front-of-house cards), eight color 11 × 14s (lobby cards) and a 40 × 60. Inside pages show other variations, as well as ads to order as cardboard mats.

◀ Not to be confused with the plain, black-and-white pressbook is this rarely produced campaign book, which like anything relating to *The Wizard of Oz* has a high value. Produced to promote maximum interest in a studio's most important releases, the campaign book was a piece of marketing in itself since its elaborate nature signaled a major promotional effort by the studio, thus prompting theaters to get out and sell it in their area. MGM was famous for using this technique during the 1930s, and this example from the original 1939 release of *Oz* is perhaps the best they produced. Measuring 18 x 16 in, it came in three full color sections, complete with tissue overlays, lobby cards, and 40-plus pages of ads and promo ideas.

▶ This press kit for the release of *The Dead Pool* in 1988 is fairly standard. Its cover is a variation on the poster art and it contains the usual printed pages with information on the film, plus eight black-and-white stills. The value of a press kit is usually determined by the number of stills included, with the average being about $3 each. Back in the 1960s, the stills sets were either a "brown bag set" of 8 to 12 (a reference to the paper envelope that housed them) or the larger (up to 40) "New York newspaper set." Huge quantities of stills were sent to the media because they were cheap to produce. Today press kits are more targeted, with large newspapers getting the greatest number of stills (but seldom more than 10) and small weeklies just one.

▶ Though titled a campaign book, this 1970 MGM-issued sales manual for *Ryan's Daughter* is a mere shadow of their earlier glorious examples. The name was revived because a new form of exhibition and distribution had evolved during the '60s. Pioneered by Twentieth Century-Fox with such hits as *The Sound of Music*, the new format, called roadshowing, presented movies on a limited basis, screening them two or three times a day with tickets sold in advance. When the films went into regular release they were usually given a major promotional send-off, hence the revival of the campaign book title.

◀ This kit for *Empire of the Sun* (1987) has a slightly higher value, despite containing only three stills, because of greater interest in the film itself. As with the pressbook, which has disappeared because of changes in film distribution and promotion, the press kit is vanishing. The stills have been replaced with a "photo cd" containing about 10 color images, plus samples of the key art, and often an image of the main poster. Some kits also have CD Roms with the trailer, soundtrack, and even games based on the film. The final death blow will be the Internet; several studios have websites from which all material can be downloaded using a password.

☆ $12–15
☆ £8–10

◄ This 1967 pressbook for *Barefoot in the Park* is notable only for the fact that it contains a sample herald (*see below left*) – a promotional device that consisted of cheaply printed flyers that theater owners could buy in quantity. They were then distributed in the lobby a week or so before the film opened. A blank space was left on the back for the theater's name and the play dates, and, appearing only on the sample, the cost information. Heralds date back to the silent era, when they were usually more colorful, and there are a handful of dedicated collectors of these ephemeral handouts. Their value is related to the film they announce but it is usually a fairly modest amount.

☆ $200–300
☆ £125–200

► The pressbook was used by several countries to promote films and this 1953 British example for *War of the Worlds* illustrates an international campaign. More elaborate than the U.S. version, its value lies not only in the interior information, but also in the use of a variation on the U.S. release poster art. But while the U.K. quad on this title has sold as high as $6,000 (slightly more than the U.S. one-sheet, which has less dramatic art), the pressbook is worth only one twentieth of that value, which indicates that these items have limited collectibility. Original pressbooks for such major films as *Frankenstein* and *The Mummy* still only fetch a fraction of the value of the one-sheets.

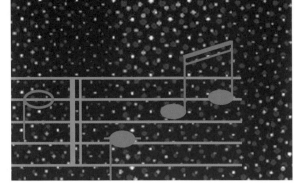

# Programs and Sheet Music

These two categories of movie ephemera are grouped together as examples of the most typical cinema souvenirs, either purchased at the theater in the case of programs or, with sheet music, bought shortly after seeing a film one wanted to remember. As with most types of collectible, keepsakes are the slowest to increase in value since they are seldom discarded, even by future generations who remember that they once meant something special to the original owner. However, exceptions abound, especially in the case of programs for films that went on to become classics but were either not box-office hits in their day or were not the type of film that really lent itself to the production of a printed memento. While the print-run of lobby programs was rather limited, sheet music was produced in vast quantities, right through to the 1950s, and even examples for such classics as "Tara's Theme" from *Gone with the Wind*, "As Time Goes By" from *Casablanca*, and "Over The Rainbow" from *The Wizard of Oz*, find market resistance to prices much above the $100 range.

▼ While almost any paper connected to *Lawrence of Arabia* (1962) tends to soar in value, the lobby program, sold during the film's initial roadshow release, is readily available at a modest price because of a warehouse find made about five years ago. The original publisher of this program, and many others, went out of business, and its immense backstock was snapped up by movie-ephemera dealers. The British version, with a different cover, then soared in value until its publisher also crashed and burned, dumping those copies onto the market.

☆ $20–25
☆ £14–17

☆ $800–1,000
☆ £525–675

▲ While most movie programs, even those from the silent era, sell for well under $100, this 40-page example from the 1941 premiere of *Citizen Kane* is an exception. Programs were invariably sold in the lobby of large downtown movie palaces only during the initial run of a film. Measuring 9 x 12 in and heavily illustrated, it is little wonder that so few exist because very few would have been sold originally. Now repeatedly cited as perhaps the greatest film ever made, *Kane* was not a box-office success on its release, neither is it the kind of heart-warming, sentimental tale that motivates audiences to buy souvenirs.

▶ The strong price for this unusually shaped *2001* first-run program is a result of the printing technology, as well as the popularity of the film. Its cover is printed in silver ink and the 24 pages are heavily illustrated, with tissue overlays. But this expensive example of '60s design overlooked the longevity factor as the metallic cover was fragile, immediately highlighting any flaws, and the lightweight paper inside could not withstand even minimal browsing. Less than 10% of those sold are in good enough condition to fetch this price.

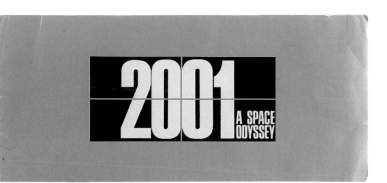

▼ Much of the success of this dark tale of deception and betrayal can be attributed to the score, which became a hit on the film's release in 1949. The relentless zither playing by Anton Karas lends a dramatic and exotic touch to the film's post-war Vienna setting. "*The Third Man Theme*", also known as "*The Harry Lime Theme*", was based on an earlier Karas piece, "*The Cafe Mozart Waltz*", named after a popular nightspot where he regularly played. Another movie edition of the score, with the same graphics, is entitled "*The Cafe Mozart Waltz*".

▲ The sheet music for *It Can't Be Wrong*, from the 1942 Bette Davis film *Now Voyager*, would ordinarily sell for under $20, but this example, which appeared at auction as part of a lot of Bette Davis ephemera a few years ago, was autographed, thus escalating the value. While this piece was authenticated by a major auction house, collectors should be wary of purchasing signed sheet music. "Autographing" sheet music was a popular party game back in the '30s and '40s, and unintentional fakes abound. A large quantity of old sheet music is lying in wait to flood the market, so prices are unlikely to increase by much.

# Stills

The motion picture was born of the technology that created photography and the movies proved family loyalty by using such quantities of still pictures that they are by far the most common film collectible available. The 8 x 10 in is the usual format (though 4 x 5 and 11 x 14 are not uncommon), and the vast majority of stills are not actual frames from a movie, but rather images shot by the unit photographer, standing in close proximity to the cameraman during production. There were also studio photographers, who would shoot standard portraits and "at home" layouts, and special photographers (such as Richard Avedon and Gordon Parks), who were hired by the publicity department to create photo stories for the major magazines in Los Angeles and New York. Each day's photography would be developed and printed into contacts (negatives laid onto photo-sensitive paper), and the stills department would pick out shots to be saved or enlarged, as would the publicity department. From the thousands of stills shot on a production, a key set of several hundred images would be selected, and placed in a special binder. This formed the basic photographic file, from which stills for the press kit, exclusive stories for major publications, and the art to be sent to National Screen for theater fronts would all be chosen.

▲ This image of Oliver Reed in the 1961 Hammer-horror film, *Curse of the Werewolf*, illustrates the commercial use of stills. The numbers on the lower right (61/133) are the same National Screen Numbers, indicating year of production and the NSS inventory number, that appear on the one-sheet and all other formats. These numbers show the still was part of a set of eight displayed in movie theaters and also sent to local newspapers. Being cheap to produce, huge quantities were created and this low guide price is typical.

▲ Color stills were quite popular in the silent era, and were almost exclusively for theater display as newspapers could only reproduce in black-and-white. However, with the rise of color sections it became possible to print color stills, as with this example from *The Bride Wore Red* (1937), and a small selection from the key set was also tinted. The color images in fan magazines and other slick publications were often specially shot, and these stills are more difficult to find.

☆ $12–15
☆ £8–10

▶ During Hollywood's golden age stars were under long-term contracts to each studio, and extensive publicity efforts were made to promote not only their individual films but the actors themselves. This photo, featuring Universal's Deanna Durbin, is a generic publicity shot, unrelated to either of the films she made in 1940 – *It's A Date* and *Spring Parade*. If it had been from one of those two films then a code, using an acronym of the title etched into the negative and thus showing in white, would have appeared in one of the lower corners. This still would have a paper caption pasted on the back; in later years publicity departments printed the captions directly onto the photo's reverse.

☆ $5–10
☆ £3–7

◀ During the 1930s and '40s the studio publicity departments would use a selection of stills from a soon-to-be released film to create a continuity layout that was sent to those newspapers that specialized in features. Called a "Story In Pictures", the set of stills (from as few as five for a B picture and up to 15 for a major release) would recreate the film's plot through captions pasted on the back. The example illustrated, from *Heartbeat* (1946) starring Eduardo Ciannelli and Ginger Rogers, shows the caption brought to the front. Vast numbers of these sets were made, and when regional newspapers closed they were thrown into the market and now appear with great regularity.

☆ $15–20
☆ £10–13

▶ As with all the stills illustrated, this 1959 *Some Like It Hot* image is from the year of the film's original release, but a large number are restrikes, made by the studio from the original negative, or from a copy negative by local media exchanges. Re-issue stills, unlike posters, are not marked, and those done soon after the first release are hard to detect. Later restrikes and blatantly fraudulent commercial copies are easier to spot since the reverse side is too smooth and white. The mild conditions of use printed along the bottom of this still have recently been made more restrictive as studios become attuned to the complexities of intellectual property law.

# Slides

It is only their inherent fragility that has prevented the glass movie slide from becoming as ubiquitous as the 8 x 10 glossie. The use of glass slides preceded the invention of movies and were a popular form of home entertainment in the late 19th century. They were also used extensively by traveling showmen, who would set up in various locations in towns and cities, projecting biblical narratives and travelogues, accompanied by a scripted lecture. In early cinemas, before a film started and, in the days before dual projectors, during reel changes, slides had a variety of purposes. They served to promote coming attractions, to create atmosphere, to advertise local shops, to project the words during a sing-along, and to instruct the audiences ("Ladies: Please Remove Your Hats"). Sadly the tens of thousands of slides that were produced were subject to breakage and even though some large quantities continue to be found, the number extant represents a tiny fraction of the total. Their golden age was the silent era, but slides were made and used right through World War II and can be found offered in many pressbooks, including that for *Casablanca* (1942). Most sell for modest values, below $20, but the highest recorded price paid was $1,400, for a film starring the escape artiste Houdini.

▲ Slides were made by contact printing a negative onto a glass plate treated with light-sensitive emulsion. The plate was then either hand-painted or stenciled, or, in some cases, left uncolored. A black paper frame was placed around the central image, another piece of glass put over the treated plate, and the entire sandwich made airtight with black paper tape around the edges. Images were drawn from the key art, often identical to the title lobby card. The slides above, from the late 1910s, are typical examples in standard condition.

▲ Dating from around 1920, this slide is perhaps the only remnant of material on this two-reeler from Fox. No paper has shown up, and even extensive research at one of the major archives is unlikely to unearth a long-neglected copy. There are thousands of lost films shot on nitrate, which was quite unstable and even dangerous when it aged, and replaced by safety film in the late 1940s. Often glass slides exist as the only record of a perished and forgotten film.

☆ $10–15
☆ £7–10

☆ $10–15
☆ £7–10

▲ ▶ These slides, made by Maurice Workstel Inc. of New York, were part of a projection system used from the late 1920s through the '30s by small and medium-sized theaters to imitate the thematic atmosphere of the giant movie palaces. Each image came as a positive and negative slide that, when projected in tandem, created a 3-D effect. The theater could be bathed in "moonlight", or made to look like a cathedral; there were even slides that projected fake curtains. Holiday themes such as Halloween were popular, as were geometric, Art Deco-style patterns.

☆ $100–150
☆ £65–100

◀ The advent of film put paid to the magic lantern circuits of traveling showmen, but the tradition of documentaries about travel became a staple of the movie industry. This slide from a 1920 film about Shackleton's South Polar adventures always sold at a slight premium because of cross-collector interest in all things related to polar exploration, but the recent flood of interest in his fantastic journey (two feature films, an Imax movie, three separate museum exhibitions, a spate of books, and three TV documentaries) has sharply escalated its value.

☆ $15–20
☆ £10–13

▶ Both glass slide and serial collectors would be interested in this 1918 example, but the low guide price is an indication of how thin a market there is for such specialized material. Eddie Polo was a famed stuntman, who started his career as a circus acrobat but was signed by Universal in 1913 and went on to become a silent-film star. *The Lure of the Circus* appeared at the height of his career and this slide, announcing the showing of the final chapter, confirms that serials were a Saturday matinee tradition from their earliest days. Polo retired in the 1930s, apart from the odd bit-part in the early 1940s.

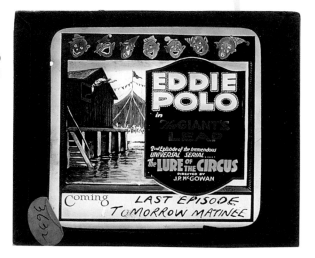

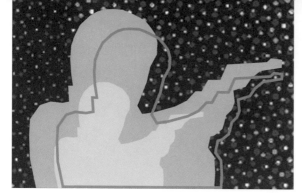

The duties associated with filling movie-theater seats fell into several departments within a major film company. The publicity staff were responsible for garnering free space in newspapers, on radio, and, in later years, TV. The advertising departments created posters and bought paid linage in newspapers, and oversaw the creation of television commercials. The promotion department sought to use other people's money to pay for ads through cooperative store displays and product tie-ins. The area most often overlooked was the warren of offices occupied by the exploitation department – those responsible for working directly with the movie theaters on "dressing" a lobby or, in the golden age of Hollywood, creating elaborate displays that, using a film's theme and key art, completely redesigned the entire front of a cinema. The term exploitation has devolved to refer only to x-rated movies, but its original use designated a group of showmen who were expert at making going to the movies an exciting event.

▲ These 40 x 80-in panels for the 1935 gangster movie, *G-Men*, are examples of lobby art – a locally generated form of theater decor. Craftsmen used the studio's basic campaign to create large decorative boards for both interior and exterior display. The images were airbrushed on pre-painted surfaces, the lettering was usually hand-cut, and large color photographs were often glued to the background. Most lobby art has been lost through endlessly recycling; this pair survived because, along with dozens of other panels, they were used in the renovation of a Boston home.

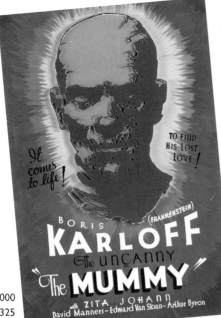

$4,000–5,000
£2,675–3,325

During the early 1930s a young illustrator, Edward Armstrong, became a lobby artist in the Atlanta area and created a body of work that survived thanks to the diligent efforts of his son. A selection was offered for sale at Christie's a few years ago and most of the items sold in the modest range that the genre usually commands. However, this gouache-on-board panel for the horror classic *The Mummy* (1932), backed by art for *A Bill of Divorcement* from the same year, sold for close to $5,000, to the same person who paid nearly half a million dollars for the horror film's one-sheet in 1997.

The 24-sheet is close to the largest regularly produced size of movie paper. Measuring 240 × 108 in, with slight variations, it comes in 12 sections (not to be confused with the rare 12-sheet), and was printed in quantities of well under 1,000 copies. It was used as a billboard by theaters that had adjacent parking lots, or displayed over the main entrance in the lobby of some of the larger downtown theaters. The relatively modest price for this huge piece of Bond paper, with one of the most sought-after images from such a major film, is due to its impractical size. But it is the ultimate paper prize for the keenest Bond collectors.

$800–1,000
£525–675

★ $30–40
★ £20–25

◀ ▼ These photos, used in the movie-trade press, show a pair of Boston theater fronts, custom-dressed for the first-run showings of *42nd Street* (1933) and the Al Jolson film, *Big Boy* (1930). They are typical of the effort that went into creating an exciting street front, and similar displays were used in hundreds of theaters across the U.S.A. At major venues on New York's Broadway or State Street, Chicago, displays the size of a city block were quite common. The *42nd Street* front is created entirely from air-brushed panels and handmade cutouts, and the *Big Boy* "poster" is really a painted sign.

★ $30–40
★ £20–25

★ $500–600
★ £325–400

◀ Just as a previous Civil War film, *The Birth of a Nation*, created a revolution in cinema exhibition by introducing the purpose-built movie house, the 1939 film *Gone with the Wind* forever changed on-site promotion of major films. So massive was its success, and so extended were its runs, that MGM produced a constant flow of promotional material to refresh the campaign and keep theater lobbies visually exciting. These four portraits, measuring 20 × 16 in, were examples of Oilette printing – a technique that created a faux oil-on-canvas appearance, previously used for reproductions of famous paintings and popular during the 1930s. So much material was produced over the long years of the initial run that, even today, one-of-a-kind items created for a specific theater turn up with some regularity.

★ $1,000–1,200
★ £675–800

▲ This illustration, 60 × 42 in, is one of a set of five that were used in the lobby of movie theaters in 1962 for *How the West Was Won* – a spectacular western filmed in the widescreen Cinerama process. While all premieres at major theaters received special treatment from the exploitation department, particular effort was made for a limited roadshow release, such as this. Only a few cinemas had the equipment to project films in the hybrid 3-D format, so this type of lobby material is quite scarce.

★ $300–400
★ £200–275

★ $400–600
★ £275–400

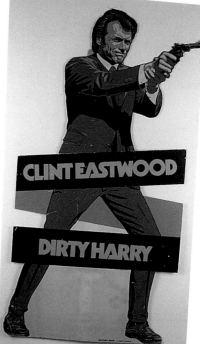

▲ The lighted lobby display has become a major promotional tool for the selling of yet-to-be-released films. The studios discovered that the relatively small but dedicated percentage of the population that attend movies regularly are a captive audience for pitches about upcoming films. Trailers are the prime device, but elaborate lobby displays are also used; this lighted standee for *Titanic* (1997) is typical, consisting of a large frame, a poster image printed on translucent plastic, and a series of fluorescent lights. It is best to buy these displays only if in unopened cartons.

▶ Spectacular and often mechanical lobby displays have been popular for the last dozen years, and cluttering the entranceway to theaters with lifesize objects is nothing new in film promotion. This 7-ft high 1971 standee for *Dirty Harry* is just one example of a tradition that goes back to the silent era. Made of heavy, pressed cardboard supported by a wooden armature, it was sent to theaters ready-assembled and must have created a startling effect. More recently theaters have given away a series of mini one-sheets for upcoming films that are becoming a popular low-end collectible – just the type of "sleeper" item that may be desirable in the future.

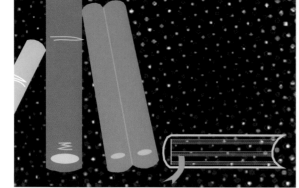

# Annuals and Film Books

Books about movies, books based on movies, and studio-issued books on movies soon-to-be-released, were once regarded as mere reference sources, or interesting support material to the hobby of collecting cinema memorabilia, but in recent years they have become collectibles in their own right, and each category has found dedicated fans. The studio-issued annual has a long history in Hollywood, dating back to the silent era, and elaborate examples were being produced right up to the demise of the classic distribution system, which required the romancing by studios of individual theater owners. Aside from being a visual treat, the annuals were filled with information about upcoming films (many of which underwent title changes or were never actually made), methods of marketing, and interesting insights into the studio's promotion of its stars. The concept of publishing a movie-edition book of a popular film started in 1912 with *The Birth of a Nation* and is still going strong, while books on movie stars, directors, history, criticism, individual films, and even books on movie collectibles, are published in a seemingly endless stream.

▼ This 1926–27 Universal Studios annual is not, as befits what was then a lesser studio, as spectacular as the Paramount example below, but it contains interesting information about Universal's serials (*Trail of the Tiger*, *Whispering Smith Rides*, and *The Fire Fighters*), and favorite stars, such as Hoot Gibson and Buster Brown. Even more fascinating are the full-page ads, which are miniatures of the one-sheets on each title. This one for *Taxi Taxi!* is signed by A.M. Froelich and, aside from a herald sold in 1992, is the only visual reference extant for this film.

☆ $60–75
☆ £40–50

☆ $200–300
☆ £125–200

▲ Issued by Paramount Studios and sent to theater owners to promote the releases of its 1925–26 season, this annual, entitled *The Golden Forty*, consists of 112 sheets printed double-sided on heavy stock. Each stone-lithographed page is a stunning example of the printer's art, with the more important films featured on two-page spreads that can stand alone as mini posters. Printing on individual sheets allowed titles to be replaced, but also meant they could go missing. Collate the pages into consecutive order, or use the list of releases usually included, to be sure all titles are present.

RKO's 1932–33 studio annual has an interesting Art Deco cover, but its relatively high value is derived from a two-page spread announcing, for the first time ever, the imminent appearance of King Kong in "The Greatest Money Picture Of The Year." Collectors of high-end posters accumulate with a passion all the ancillary ephemera associated with their prize: the Universal annuals that announce *Frankenstein* or *The Mummy* sell into the thousands. In the 1930s MGM produced a series entitled *The Lion's Roar*, the one to announce *Gone with the Wind* is the most prized.

☆ $1,200–1,500
☆ £800–1,000

☆ $6–8
☆ £4–5

☆ $80–100
☆ £55–65

Starting in 1969 with *Ninotchka*, to *Alien* in 1979, Richard Anobile edited a series of large-format books that reconstructed famous films, not from stills, but by using actual frames from a print of the film. In most cases the images start with the credits and each frame is captioned by excerpts from the script. The 1974 *Frankenstein* edition has over 1,000 images and is the most sought-after. Once easily found at low prices, values have escalated as collectors vie for a full set.

Published in 1944, this movie edition of *Jane Eyre* is simply the original novel in a new dust jacket. Such editions have a low collectiblility value; more sought-after are those that intersperse text with stills from the film. The most noted, and first, of the post-silent films to receive this treatment was *Gone with the Wind*. Its 1940 movie edition was produced in vast quantities, but the few in excellent condition fetch $50. Re-issued books of recent films, with the key art on the cover, are gaining value, first editions and pristine condition being paramount wants.

☆ $900–1,200
☆ £600–800

This page advertising Fritz Lang's *Metropolis* is from the 1926–27 *Paramount Pictures 15th Birthday Production Yearbook*. Having acquired the German sci-fi film, the U.S. studio did not know how to promote a film featuring a beautiful robot and a mad scientist, living in a city powered by industrial slaves about to revolt. If this initial campaign had survived, audiences expecting a light, sophisticated comedy would have been in for a shock. This first appearance of release information on such a major film drives up the price of an already valuable annual.

# Miscellaneous Promotional Items

☆ $10–15
☆ £7–10

The story is told of a staff meeting called by a vice president in charge of advertising, publicity, promotion, and exploitation back in the 1960s. Holding up a copy of the *New York Sunday Times* he pointed to a full-page ad for one of the studio's current releases and uttered "$12,000"; he then turned to a large feature story, complete with photos and said the word "free." The press agent who had planted the story noted that if you count the martini-soaked lunch at Sardi's with the editor, it wasn't completely free. The message is that, following the paid advertising, promoting a film is all about leveraging small costs into large results, and creating attention-grabbing objects is a cheap way to garner attention for a movie release. "Promotional items" is a catch-all term for gewgaws and gimmicks produced by the teams working to sell a film. The publicity staff usually design items aimed at the press, while other departments create give-aways to be used in movie theaters, and cross-promotions with manufacturers, imprinting the name of the film on everything from lunch boxes to bathing suits. With the rise of modern licensing, toy stores often have half their shelf-space devoted to movie tie-ins and fast-food venues are saturated with throwaways for current releases. It will be many years before these contemporary promos achieve any meaningful collectible value.

▲ Presenting a comic book as a promotional item for a film based on a comic book is not only lazy, it's a very ineffective way of attracting attention to a movie. Many films have used comics as promos (*Close Encounters of the Third Kind*, *Jay, Silent Bob,* and *Jurassic Park*) but, as their minor collectible value indicates, they cause little excitement at a movie's release, as was so with this 3-D comic for *Rocketeer* (1991). Promo collectors are wary of the huge quantity of comics produced, and comic-book fans regard them with disdain.

☆ $4–5
☆ £3–4

▲ The creation of "nerf", a spongy plastic substance that weighs almost nothing and can be molded into a seemingly infinite variety of shapes, has inspired many studio publicity departments. There are nerf footballs (*Varsity Blues*), a nerf mouse (*AntiTrust*), and hats, clowns, and tiaras galore. They are minor collectibles, but most have the film's name emblazoned on them. It's hard to guess the title of this film (the 1999 comedy *Pushing Tin*, about air traffic controllers) as the item is so generic it could just as well have been for the classic comedy *Airplane*. The first rule of promos is that they clearly represent the film in question.

☆ $1,500–2,000
☆ £1,000–1,325

▲ ▶ There are no known promo items from the three Universal "mega-movies" of the early 1930s (*Frankenstein*, *Dracula*, and *The Mummy*), but RKO was more aggressive in its marketing of the fourth film in what has come to be known as "The Killer Quartet." *King Kong* was released in 1933 and its studio made a major selling effort, evidenced by the press book on the title. Done in color (unusual at any time), it pictured all the posters available, plus copious suggestions as to how theaters could gain maximum publicity. One such method was the jigsaw puzzle, which enjoyed a faddish boom in the early Depression and was a popular advertising tool. This Kong puzzle is the only one ever found in near-pristine condition, complete with envelope.

☆ $20–25
☆ £13–17

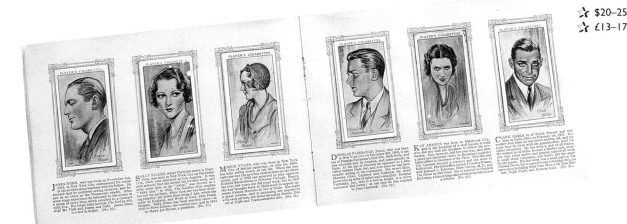

▲ Collecting cigarette cards on a wide variety of themes was one of the most popular hobbies in Britain during a large part of the 20th century. Ironically it was an American invention, dating from the late 19th century, which was taken up abroad just as the huge U.S. tobacco companies abandoned it as a marketing tool. During the 1930s several major British firms, such as Player's and Wills, issued cards of movie stars. Those above are part of a set of 50, which could be glued in an album available for just a few pence. The cards were quite desirable and seemingly scarce, with prices rising close to $100 a set, until the intervention of Internet auctions; the now constant supply has driven down the value. As tobacco-card collectibles they are worth more unmounted, but as film ephemera the opposite is true.

Just when you thought it was safe to go back to the refreshment stand, your soft drink comes in a *Coca Cola/Jaws* cross-promotion tie-in plastic drinking cup! The late '70s marked the beginning of the massive cooperative merchandising of movies, and this *Jaws 2* (1977) cup is an early example of what has now become a staple of every movie's exploitation schedule. Anything from popcorn tubs to candy wrappers is used, and all major films have a heatedly negotiated arrangement with either McDonalds or Burger King to promote using their trinkets.

☆ $8–10
☆ £5–7

The 1990s marked the era of the promotional t-shirt. Practically every film with more than a modest budget had one created for it along with a cap and, for the higher-end productions, such items as baseball jackets, gym shirts, and other casual clothing. These mass-produced items are not to be confused with "crew jackets", which are high-quality, quite expensive, and produced in a limited amount only. They are given to cast and crew members, usually at the end of production, and show a discreet, or discreet in Hollywood terms, logo from the film.

☆ $12–15
☆ £8–10

☆ $25–30
☆ £17–20

Those responsible for promotions at film studios are always on the lookout for new items to sate the jaded tastes of the reviewers and editors, who are constantly inundated with presents bearing film images and titles. This millennium countdown clock was adapted to promote the sci-fi picture *Armageddon* (1998). As with most trendy promo items, the first few sold for a very high price (up to $100/£65), but as more and more were made the market collapsed. It is often a seller's market at the onset so let prices settle down before jumping in.

☆ $1–2
☆ 50p–£1

▶ Marking the low end of promotional material, these transfers or temporary tattoos have become popular giveaways. No longer satisfied to have the public as walking advertisements by just wearing t-shirts and baseball caps, the studios now entice youngsters to decorate their flesh to promote their films! The diverse movies represented here, *Dude Where's My Car*, *Dungeons and Dragons*, and *Traffic* (all from 2000), give an idea of how wide the promoters throw their net. Other cheap items, such as postcards and key chains, are produced in vast quantities and their distribution is not limited to those in the media since they are often given away at theaters prior to a film's premiere. They seldom attain any value as collectibles.

☆ $12–15
☆ £8–10

◀ Soundtrack albums have always been significant promotional items for the major movie studios. They represent an important cross-over promotion with record companies, who often create elaborate displays in music stores, thus reaching young people, the prime movie-going audience, in yet another venue. But they seldom rise to any great value, and this soundtrack CD from *Bedazzled* (2000) is no exception. For a brief period in the mid '90s the film studios (in particular Disney) were creating entire press kits on CDs. Many thought it marked the end of the printed version, but reviewers resisted and the paper and ink variety still reigns (see pp.106–109). The press kit CDs were packaged to resemble the soundtracks and they sell at a premium – up to $50/£35 each.

ORIGINAL MOTION PICTURE SOUNDTRACK
ELIZABETH HURLEY
BRENDAN FRASER

Meet the Devil.
She's giving Elliott
seven wishes.
But not a chance
in Hell.

BEDAZZLED

# Autographs

⭐ $600–800
⭐ £400–525

The authors of this book have been associated with the U.S. version of *Antiques Roadshow* since its first appearance in 1995, one as a generalist expert and one as a specialist in entertainment memorabilia. In that time they have seen thousands upon thousands of autographs and that huge number does not touch the quantity seen by other appraisers on the show. As with other collectibles that appear in large numbers (quality animation cels, for example), if all this material were released to the marketplace, values would crumble. That is just one of the dangers associated with autograph collecting; while out-and-out fakes abound, even more troublesome are the high percentage of "secretary-signed" examples. Major personalities, be they movie stars, musicians, stage actors, or statesmen, did not have time to answer all their mail and assistants most often sent back thoughtfully personalized signatures. This is one area where only the advanced collector should tread alone – others should pay the higher prices demanded by top dealers and major auction houses, who stand behind their authentication, and regard the extra money as an insurance premium.

⭐ $200–300
⭐ £125–200

▲ These two photos appeared at Christie's, New York, in December 2000 and, judging by the catalog entries, the specialist in charge did an excellent job of authenticating them. With any autograph the first test is to compare it with the signature as it appears in the many samplers available for sale; these books contain page after page of signatures of a huge number of personalities. Once it is confirmed, attempt to date it: in the case of the Astaire/Rogers photo the caption material from the studio mentions a specific film (*Roberta*, 1935); and the dedication "To Madeline" on the Joan Crawford photo is helpful as the ubiquitous Madeline was a minor stage actress of the '30s and '40s who spent her time obtaining the signatures of the rich and famous.

The envelope pictured is part of a lot consisting of three Jean Seberg typewritten letters, all signed by the famed actress, complete with envelopes. They discuss daily life with Seberg's husband, the author Romain Gary, during the summer of 1965. The texts also mention the darker side of Jean Seberg's life at this time, when she was investigated by the C.I.A. for possible "un-American" activities. Also included is a holographic thank you note and an undated gift card in her handwriting. The lot appeared at auction in Boston in 1999 with an estimate of $7,000–9,000 and failed to sell. The high valuation was due to a stiff reserve (the price below which the consignor will not go); the guide price, left, is far more realistic.

☆ $2,000–3,000
☆ £1,325–2,000

☆ $100–200
☆ £65–125

▶ The Mary Tyler Moore Show is regarded as a TV classic and, of all the broadcasts, the episode usually referred to as "Chuckles The Clown", but actually titled "Chuckles Bites The Dust", is undoubtedly the best-remembered. The low estimate on this artifact is not in any way due to doubts about the authenticity of Moore's signature (which was established when it came up for auction in Boston several years ago), but rather to the fact that autographed TV scripts are quite common. For years the various public television stations in the U.S.A. would entreat celebrities to submit autographed items to the fund-raising auctions they held every year and invariably a signed script would be sent to satisfy the request; in some cases entire casts would sign (for example those of M.A.S.H. and Cheers). Over time a large number have become available, driving down prices.

◀ This Italian photobusta from Lawrence of Arabia (1962) is a desirable collectible in itself, but would be worth less than $300 without Peter O'Toole's signature. When it came up for sale at a London auction, it was accompanied by a set of contact prints showing the star actually signing the poster. Going to such lengths to authenticate is not unheard of, and in this case it escalated the value in proportion to the energy expended. But be wary of attempts at establishing provenance using elaborate affidavits and testimonials, complete with stamps and seals – simple proofs can be more reliable.

☆ $600–800
☆ £400–525

☆ $1,000–2,000
☆ £675–1,325

◀ At the end of each workday, Walt Disney would repair to a special desk where his correspondence was laid out and, with flourishes and bold strokes, would sign his mail, but he almost never signed requests for autographs (except to top politicians and heads of state). Neither, from the late '20s, did he draw Mickey Mouse, despite the number of examples that appear. However, he did sign in public when cornered, as evidenced by this menu from a 1964 dinner in Mexico signed by Disney, President Eisenhower, and his brother, John. Such "accumulation" items can be of less value, since few people collect both Disney and Ike material.

◀ This 1939 "rainbow" (final continuity shooting script) for the classic John Wayne film *Stagecoach* is signed on its cover by the director, John Ford, and its producer, Walter Wanger. Included when this item was sold at auction in 1999 was a letter to a film critic at a major Texas newspaper from John Le Roy Johnson, Director of Publicity at United Artists, dated 21 August 1939, that stated, in part: "Since the script is really our stock in trade one seldom ever leaves the studio, so you may feel complimented in possessing the only copy of 'Stagecoach' to leave the files." Authentic beyond a doubt, this major artifact of film history was purchased by one of the industry's leading directors.

☆ $9,000–10,000
☆ £6,000–6,675

▶ The lowliest form of autograph is a signature scrawled on a plain piece of paper grabbed in desperation when a famous person is trapped in a public place. But this taped and tattered shred bears the signature of James Dean – mega-icon, and infamous "non-signer", who departed this world before he had a chance, unlike Elvis Presley, to sign thousands of such scraps. Also at the lower end of the scale are autograph-album pages. These are usually bought in bulk by dealers, mated with an appropriate, but not always original, photograph and sold at a handsome price that is rarely recoverable through re-sale.

☆ $1,000–1,200
☆ £675–800

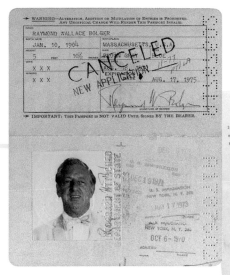

▶ Checks, passports, and contracts are popular autograph sources since they are guaranteed to be authentic, although most Hollywood stars and prominent figures do not sign their own checks because many are not cashed, leaving them open to possible legal complications. The problem with mundane items such as this Ray Bolger passport is the lack of association with the star's career, but "completists", who collect anything they can get on their favorite subject, are perfect dealer fodder for this type of material. Contracts, often containing interesting demands, are more sought-after; this Clark Gable document for his 1959 film, *But Not for Me*, supplies such details as his salary ($25,000) in its 47 pages.

◀ These two photos were part of a large lot of ephemera auctioned off by an author, who had acquired them as source material for a biography of Liza Minnelli. The value, of course, lies with the Garland signed photo, but the young Liza picture also presents an interesting opportunity for autograph collectors. Many in the hobby send photos to stars, complete with return address envelopes, requesting signatures. It is felt that the more interesting a photo sent, the more likely it will be signed and returned, so this offbeat image might earn a response.

☆ $1,200–1,400
☆ £800–925

There existed a long tradition in Hollywood of actors and crew members taking home a piece of property from a production as a souvenir, but what had been an almost private market among members of the film community exploded into what has become a collectibles mini-industry in 1971 when Twentieth Century-Fox held its famous backlot auction. Over a period of weeks the giant studio divested itself of thousands upon thousands of items from its huge archive. Working from a series of catalogs issued by Sotheby's, a team of auctioneers emptied warehouses full of memorabilia that had been used over and over again in Fox films down the years. This treasure trove formed the basis of a new hobby, and now all the major auction houses hold regular sales of similar material and the Internet is awash with offers of props from current films. The intense interest in owning an actual item used by a famed star in a major film has naturally caused some questions of authenticity. Out and out fakes exist, but the existence of duplicates doesn't necessarily indicate fraud. With most smaller props several versions are made, and there are also backups created, but it is still best to buy any high-price items from a reputable dealer or auctioneer.

☆ $10,000–12,000
☆ £6,675–8,000

▲ These items from Mel Brooks' 1967 comedy *The Producers* were sold at auction several years ago for about 80 per cent of the guide price indicated here, but the higher estimate is a result of the frenzy surrounding the recent Broadway adaptation. Prop-collecting has become a vast hobby, and posters that were created for use within films are popular: this three-sheet was outside the theater on the opening night of the fictitious *Springtime For Hitler*. When this copy was sold it was the only one known to exist, but another has been found and it seems that of the 100 printed 97 were pulped, so there may be a third one out there. The prop "playbill" (top) survived in the classic manner – an extra in the movie kept it as a souvenir.

☆ $150,000–165,000
☆ £100,000–110,000

◀ Charlie Chaplin items attract high prices, but with such a small, ardent group of aficionados the danger of the buyer-end of the market thinning is always present. However, recent sales are holding their own as a few new collectors enter the fray, including some institutions. This hat, cane, and pair of shoes from his roles as "the little tramp" were bought several years ago so the value-estimate may be only a starting price. There has been a recent spate of Chaplin props at auctions, the cane in particular, but none with such bullet-proof provenance.

▼ There have been huge auctions devoted solely to Marilyn Monroe collectibles, and every major sale of movie memorabilia contains a section of dresses, props, and objects with, often very tenuous, connections to the mega-star. This 1954 black-and-white photo, by Bruno Bernard, was sold at Christie's, New York, in May 2000. The lot contained other ephemera related to Bernard, but it was this famed photo from *The Seven Year Itch* that the bidders were after. Never-before-seen photos of Monroe, recovered from photographer's estates, fetch consistently high prices at auction.

☆ $500,000–600,000
☆ £335,000–400,000

☆ $8,000–10,000
☆ £5,325–6,675

▲ The highest prize Hollywood can offer an actor is the Academy Award, and the Oscar statuette is often just as prized by movie collectors. The Academy has made many attempts to block the sale of the awards, but consignors and auction houses have conspired to find loopholes and have benefited from all the resulting publicity. This Oscar, awarded to Bette Davis for her starring role in *Jezebel* (1938), was sold to Steven Spielberg for nearly $600,000 at Christie's, New York, in July 2001. He has bought several Oscars and donated them to the Academy of Motion Pictures, Arts, and Sciences, thus closing the publicity loop.

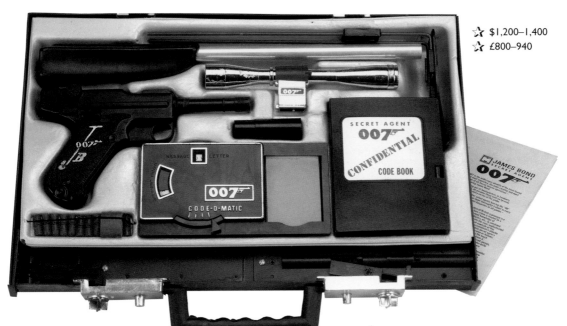

★ $1,200–1,400
★ £800–940

Once in a while avid James Bond fans gather to take part in a feeding frenzy of bidding that would be more at home in Blofeld's piranha pool than the elegant rooms of an auction house. Everything from perfectly packaged and preserved dinky toys to actual autos used in the films are on offer. This 007 Secret Agent Shooting Attaché Case, from a 2001 sale at Christie's, South Kensington, is in pristine condition – totally complete, and intact – and went for the higher end of its guide price. Issued in 1965, near the start of the Bond film cycle, it is the type of complicated toy that finds favor with this film series' collectors.

★ $2,000–2,500
★ £1,325–1,675

Frank Sinatra played the private detective Tony Rome twice, once in the film by that name which appeared in 1967 and again in *Lady in Cement* (1968), opposite Raquel Welch. These two studio-created pieces of ID were used in the first film and were so seemingly authentic that it states on the reverse of one of the cards that it is to be used only as a prop in a motion picture. In typical Hollywood style, the typed information is not quite accurate: the height and weight aren't far off, but of course the eye color is wrong, the age is nine years too young, and while the hair at the time of the photo might have been brown, by this time in his career Sinatra could change that just by shaking out a new rug.

▶ These large doors, nearly eight feet tall, are seen again and again in scenes from *Casablanca* (1942) as the entrance to Rick's gambling den. Made of wood, they are painted orange, rust, and brown, but since the original film was in black and white it is hard to know if these are the original colors. At a New York auction in July 2001 they sold for $41,125. Seven years before, at a similar auction, they had fetched $20,700 – not a bad investment, plus one must assume that the owner had several years of enjoyment from owning a major prop from one of the all-time movie classics.

$14,000–16,000
£9,325–10,675

◀ When Charlton Heston as Moses descends from Mount Sinai in the film *The Ten Commandments* this golden calf, measuring 6 × 6 ft, is prominently on view. Such huge props are seldom bought by individuals for their own use and tend to end up decorating themed restaurants or gambling casinos. Made of wood and painted with gold leaf it is a bit worse for wear, but it still managed to sell at the upper end of the guide price in a recent auction, as did seven other major props from this 1956 epic, helped by the inclusion of stills from the film that prominently displayed them.

$800–1,000
£525–675

▶ Director's chairs with a famous name stenciled on the canvas back have long been popular with collectors, but they have been just as popular with fakers, and even the studio hands who made them have been known to produce a few extra for re-sale. This chair appeared at auction in 2000 and the catalog entry is a masterpiece of non-attribution: "a metal folding chair with 'Gloria Swanson, Sunset Boulevard, 1949' printed on the backrest." Nowhere does it state that it was actually used by Swanson during the film, and the "1949" is a strong clue that this was a post-production cast-and-crew souvenir. A chair used by Swanson in this movie would be worth far more.

$5,000–6,000
£3,325–4,000

◀ Hollywood props, like California wine, can miraculously become vintage within a year. This axe from *Gladiator* (2000) was sold at Christie's in 2001. Attending the auction previews of such sales can be enlightening and amusing – upon inspection, this sinister weapon turns out to be made of hard rubber gilded in metal paint. It was estimated at $1,200–1,400 but fetched nearer $6,000. Auction estimates of such possibly unique items are often just guesses by the auction house, which prefers to err on the lower side so as to encourage opening bids. Of course the consignor wants higher estimates, since his reserve price (the least he will accept) is slightly below the lower estimate. The presence of a photo from the film, while usually not included in the lot, invariably helps sell an item.

▶ Props often fare better at auction if they are closely related to the theme and mood of a film. This light-up neon umbrella from *Blade Runner* is just one of many that are seen throughout the 1982 film, which was shot in a shrouded mist. The lot also had several other plus factors working for it: the film is a cult favorite and most items, from posters to props, always do well; the item was illustrated by a color photo from the film with a row of umbrellas prominently visible; the lot also included a letter of authenticity from a member of the movie production team. However, be careful when buying items that were produced in multiples for use during filming, as the possibility of numerous "back-ups" can cause the value to plummet.

$2,000–3,000
£1,325–2,000

Personal items related to a movie star are often hard to come by, and usually only appeal to the specialized collector. This selection of original photos appeared at auction in 1999. The lot consisted of five 4 x 6 in photographs, dating from 1906–1915 and featuring a very young Fred Astaire with his sister Adele, and a holograph letter penned by their father, Fred E. Astaire, using both that name and his real name, Fritz Austerlitz. The children were vaudeville stars and the letter details their career to date and future plans. Despite the photos appearing in several Fred Astaire biographies the lot struggled to reach $1,000. Astaire's fans, it seems, prefer material related to his image as a suave and debonair dancer.

★ $800–1,000
★ £525–675

Film costumes are a major part of prop collectibles, but a secure provenance is a must. Even major auction houses have been duped by clever forgerers, though more recently frauds have been spotted at previews by one of the large number of well-informed collectors. A sewn-in label with the film title, production number, and sometimes the actor's name is an aid. This lot from *Ben Hur* (1958) was shown with the lobby card, above, depicting Charlton Heston in the caftan. If no photo exists, look for a still or poster that displays the item.

★ $2,000–3,000
★ £1,325–2,000

The before-and-after images of the one-sheet for *Rain Man* (opposite) illustrate the dramatic results of poster restoration. On the left the poster is shown unrestored, but in the photo on the right it has been "linen-mounted" – a misnomer in fact since the backing substance is actually duck canvas. (The term is a hold-over from the early 20th century for a French process of paper conservation.) The canvas is a natural, acid-free substance, as is the light paper placed behind the poster and the wheat paste used as an adherent. Thus mounted a poster can then be restored. In this case, the major work (done by M. & W. Graphics of New York) involved painstakingly painting out the fold lines and treating a few paper cracks around the edges. As an indication of the value of restoration, the unrestored poster was worth about $25 but mounted and lightly restored it sells for close to $300. A restorer can do much work on a poster, piecing together paper-loss areas and painting in entire sections, but a controversy has been raging in the movie-poster world about exactly how much restoration is proper.

In the early 1990s, when the boom in movie collecting started, collectors were far more forgiving of major restoration since it was felt that movie posters had suffered a hard career, traveling from theater to theater, being folded and unfolded, and tacked to display boards, etc. Also, because very little information existed, it was often believed that the poster on view at an auction was the only surviving example. Much damage was done in the name of salvation and a number of posters were massively and irrevocably restored. The same standards are now applied to movie paper as to other genres of poster such as travel or war – that only the absolute minimum of restoration is acceptable. Many collectors are eschewing mounting altogether or, if it is done, allowing only the deacidifying process, which has a stabilizing influence. However, poster dealers are particularly fond of the mounting process since it makes their inventory easier to handle and display, and some of the less scrupulous use the method to mask major flaws. If possible, hold the poster up to a strong light and major restoration should be visible. Large "inpainted" areas can often be felt by touching the surface, or they become apparent when the poster is looked at in reflected light from different angles. Many of the over-restored posters from ten years ago are hiding in dealers' inventories, waiting to be landed on unsuspecting neophytes. They are not fakes or frauds as such, but posters that should be graded perhaps a B or B-. This letter scale of grading is used by auction houses and most dealers: the letter A indicates a poster that is pristine, unmounted, and unrestored – a very rare rating indeed; A- denotes an excellent poster, still unrestored but perhaps mounted; all posters which have any work done to them are automatically considered B+, and the grading descends from there, indicating the amount of pinholes or tears, for example.

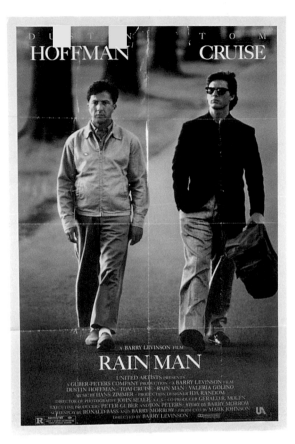

Many poster buyers object to the fold lines in pre-1990 posters (from that time almost all were sent to theaters rolled), which is especially a problem with posters from the late 1970s and '80s that were printed on glossy stock, as with the *Rain Man* example above. The fold lines tended to separate and become more obvious than on older posters printed on untreated paper. Currently, removing these marks is still acceptable but the PC (Paper Conservation) police might start to crack down on that as well.

Linen-backing is fine for one-sheets and other posters on lighter paper, but window cards, lobby cards, and other formats on light card stock should be backed with Japan paper – a slightly more expensive process. Restoration in general

is not overly expensive: simply mounting a poster runs to about $40–50, and restoration work is charged at an average hourly rate of $35 (£25). When getting a poster framed demand archival treatment, which requires that everything be acid-free and inert, including the backing and any hinging tape or matting material used. The poster must not touch the glass, or plexiglass, so ask that "spacers" be inserted to keep them apart.

Unmounted posters must be kept away from heat, dampness, and light (as the "fugitive colors", especially reds, are washed out by sunlight). Laying the posters flat in a pile, interleaved with sheets of acid-free paper, with a light weight on top, not only preserves them but helps to reduce the undesirable fold marks.

# Bibliography

Borst, Ronald, V., *Graven Images: The Best of Horror, Fantasy and Science Fiction Film Art*, Grove Press, 1992

Choko, Stanislas, *100 Ans d'Affiches de Cinéma*, Paris, 1995

Cuthbertson, Rod, *Movie Poster Art*, Privately printed, Australia, 2001

Dydo, Krzysztof, *Polish Film Poster: 100th Anniversary of the Cinema in Poland, 1896–1996*, Exhibition Catalog, 1996

Edwards, Gregory, J., *The Book of the International Film Poster*, Tiger Books International, 1985

Kisch, John, *Movie Poster Price Almanac*, Hyde Park, 2001

Kisch, John and Mapp, Edward, *A Separate Cinema*, Farrar, Straus & Giroux, 1992

Kowalski, Tadeusz, *The Polish Film Poster*, Filmowa Agencja Wydawnicza, 1957

Michel, Albin, *Ferracci: Affichiste de Cinéma*, Paris, 1991

Miller, Frank, *MGM Posters: The Golden Years*, J.G. Press, 1998

Nixdorf, Thomas, *Licence to Thrill: James Bond Plakate, 1962-1992*, Hannover, 1997

Pack, Susan, *Film Posters of the Russian Avant-Garde*, Taschen America, 1995

Rebello, Stephen and Allen, Richard, *Reel Art: Great Posters from the Golden Age of the Silver Screen*, Abbeville Press, 1992

Schapiro, Steve and Chierichetti, David, *The Movie Poster Book*, E. P. Dutton, 1979

Stallaerts, Rik and de Hert, Robbe, *Prochainement dans cette salle : chronique de l'affiche de cinéma belge*, Gand, 1995

Steffens, Horst et al, *Im Auftraf Hollywoods: Filmplakate aus 40 Jahren von "Peltzer"*, Germany, 1995

Studio Canal, *Un demi siécle de cinéma à Cannes*, Privately printed, 2000

Wolff, Mark, H. and Nourmand, Tony, ed., *Hitchcock Poster Art: From the Mark H. Wolff Collection*, Overlook Press, 1999

Wright, Bruce Lanier, *Yesterday's Tomorrows: The Golden Age of Science Fiction Movie Posters*, Taylor Publishing Company, 1993

Zreik, Serge, *Les Affiches de la Nouvelle Vague 1958–1969*, Biarritz, 1998

# Sources and Resources

## Shops:

**At The Movies**

Antiquarius Antiques Market
135 Kings Road
London SW3 8DT, UK
Tel: (0044) 20 7376 7670
www.originalfilmposters.com

**Hollywood Canteen**

1516 Danforth, Toronto
Ontario M4J 1N4, Canada
Tel: (001) 416 461 1704

**Intemporel**

22 Rue St Martin
Paris 75004, France
Tel: (0033) 42 72 5541
www.choko.net

**Motion Picture Arts Gallery**

133 East 58th Street
New York, NY 10022, USA
Tel: (001) 212 223 1009
www.mpagallery.com

**The Nostalgia Factory**

51 North Margin Street
Boston, MA 02113, USA
Tel: (001) 800 479 8754
www.nostalgia.com

**Posteritati**

241 Centre Street
New York
NY 10013, USA
Tel: (001) 212 226 2207
www.posteritati.com

**Reel Poster Gallery**
72 Westbourne Grove
London W2 5SH, UK
Tel: (0044) 20 7727 4488
www.reelposter.com

**Dealers on the Web/E-mail:**
**Cinegrafix**
(UK, European posters)
www.rarefilmposters.com

**Jim Dietz**
(American classics, French posters)
www.jimdietz.com

**John Hazelton**
(Strong general selection)
www.filmposters.com

**Alexis Rubinowicz**
(French posters)
rubi@cybercable.fr

**Separate Cinema**
(Black film material)
www.separate.cinema.com

**Movie news, information:**
*Movie Collectors World*
(Monthly trade paper for film
posters and autographs)
Box 309, Fraser
MI 48026, USA
Tel: (001) 810 774 4311
www.mcwonline.com

**Internet Movie Database**
(Movie credits, production info)
www.imdb.com

**www.posterprice.com**
(Invaluable site for movie poster
collectors: prices, news, dealers)

**www.film.com**
(Home of MOPO – lively online
movie-poster discussion group)

**Auctioneers:**
**Christie's New York**
20 Rockefeller Plaza
New York
NY 10020, USA
Tel: (001) 212 636 2000
www.christies.com
(Contact Margaret Barrett – props,
posters, autographs, memorabilia)

**Christie's South Kensington**
85 Old Brompton Road
London SW7 3LD, UK
Tel: (0044) 20 7321 3281
www.christies.com
(Contact Sarah Hodgson – props,
posters, autographs, memorabilia)
Both have several memorabilia
sales a year with valuable catalogs

**www.ebay.com**
(Search for movie posters,
autographs, props, etc.)

**Skinner Inc. Auctioneers
& Appraisers of Antiques &
Fine Art**
357 Main Street, Bolton
MA 01740, USA
Tel: (001) 978 779 6241
www.skinnerinc.com

**Supplies/Restoration:**
**Bags Unlimited**
(Everything needed for poster
presentation and display)
7 Canal Street
Rochester
NY 14608, USA
Tel: (001) 800 767 BAGS (2247)
www.bagsunlimited.com

**M & W Graphics**
(Linenbackers and restorers)
37 West 20th Street
New York
NY 10011, USA
Tel: (001) 212 727 8320

**Fairs:**
**Les Cingles Du Cinéma**
(An annual film poster "orgy",
last weekend of January in
the Paris suburb of Argenteuil,
open from 2pm Friday)
Tel: (0033) 39 61 01 50

**Collectors Film Convention**
(Occurs six times a year in
central London – posters,
autographs, and a great
atmosphere)
Tel: Ed Mason on
(0044) 20 736 8511

**Vintage Poster Show
(and auction)**
(The annual major U.S. vintage
poster event, in late May,
in Columbus, Ohio)
www.vintagefilmposters.com

# Index

Acknowledgments

**Thanks to:** Dan Farrell, *Antiques Roadshow* appraiser wrangler extraordinaire, who said the magic words that caused all these words to appear in print; Emily Anderson of Miller's, who saw us through dangers and deadlines, edited our verbosity and punctured our pomposity; Karen Keane of Skinner Inc. Auctioneers and her wizard staff for all the help with images; and Margaret Barrett of Christie's New York who made the props section so bright and cheery.

**Picture credits:** Front of Jacket (clockwise from top left): SK, SK, SK, OPG; Back of Jacket: SK; Half-title: CI; 2: CI; 3: CI; 7: CI; 8: CI; 10: CI; 11: CI; 12: CI; 13t: SK; 13cl: CI; 13br: OPG; 14t: SK; 14cl: CI; 14cr: CI; 15: CI; 16tl: CI; 16tr: SK; 16b: SK; 17 tl: CI; 17tr: OPG; 17br: OPG; 18t: CI; 18b: OPG; 19: SK; 20tl: CI; 20tr: CI; 20br: SK; 21tr: CI; 21bl: SK; 22: CI; 23: CI; 24: CI; 25 tr: OPG; 25tl: OPG; 25cr: CI; 25bl: CI; 26: SK; 27: SK; 28: SK; 29t: SK; 29cr: SK; 29bl: OPG; 30tl: SK; 30cr: OPG; 30bl: OPG; 31: SK; 32tl: OPG; 32br: CI; 33: SK; 34: SK; 35: SK; 36: OPG; 37tr: SK; 37cl: SK; 37br: OPG; 38: CI; 39: CI; 40: SK; 41: SK; 42l: CI; 42r: SK; 43tr: CI; 43bl: OPG; 44: SK; 45tl: OPG; 45cr: SK; 45bl: SK; 46tl: CI; 46bl: SK; 46br: CLA; 47tr: OPG; 47bl: CI; 47br: CI; 48tr: SC; 48bl: SK; 49tl: OPG; 49tr: SC; 49cr: SK; 49bl: CI; 50: CI; 51tl: SK; 51cr: SK; 51bl: CI; 52t: CI; 52b: OPG; 53tr: SK; 53cl: OPG; 53br: OPG; 54tl: CI; 54cr: CI; 54bl: B; 55: CI; 56: SK; 57tr: CI; 57cl: CI; 57br: SK; 58t: CI; 58bl: SK; 58br: SK; 59: SK; 60: SK; 61: SK; 62: OPG; 63: SK; 64: SK; 65: SK; 66tr: CI; 66bl: SK; 67: SK; 68: SK; 69: SK; 70: SK; 71: SK; 72: SK; 73t: OPG; 73b: CI; 74t: CI; 75tl: SK; 75cr: OPG; 75bl: OPG; 76: SK; 77tl: OPG; 77cr: CI; 77bl: CI; 78: CI; 79: CI; 80tl: OPG; 80br: SK; 81tr: SK; 81cl: OPG; 81br: SK; 82: OPG; 83tl: OPG; 83cl: OPG; 83cr: SK; 84: SK; 85: SK; 86: SK; 87tr: CI; 87cl: SK; 87br: SK; 88: SK; 89: SK; 90: OPG; 91: SK; 92: CI; 93tr: OPG; 93cl: SK; 93br: CI; 94: SK; 95tl: OPG; 95cr: CI; 95bl: OPG; 96: OPG; 97: OPG; 98: CI; 99: SK; 100: OPG; 101: OPG; 102t: CI; 102b: SK; 103tl: CI; 103tr: CI; 103c: CI; 103b: SK; 104: CI; 106: OPG; 107t: CI; 107b: OPG; 108: OPG; 109t: OPG; 109cl: OPG; 109br: CI; 110t:OPG; 110b: SK; 111tr: OPG; 111cl: SK; 111br: OPG; 112t: 1961 Universal-International; 112b: Franchi; 113t: Universal Pictures Co. Inc.; 113cl: Franchi; 113br: 1959 United Artists Corporation; 114: OPG; 115: OPG; 116: SK; 117: CI; 118t: Franchi; 118c: Franchi; 118b: SK; 119tr: CI; 119cl: SK; 119br: SK; 120: OPG; 121t: SK; 121cl: OPG; 121cr: OPG; 121br: CI; 122: OPG; 123t: SK; 123b: OPG; 124: OPG; 125: OPG; 126: CI; 127tl: SK; 127cr: SK; 127bl: CI; 128t: CI; 128c: SK; 128b: CI; 129t: CI; 129b: SK; 130t: CI; 130b: SK; 131: CI; 132t: Glidrose Productions Ltd/EON Productions Ltd/CI; 132b: CI; 133: CI; 134: CI; 135t: SK; 135b: CI; 137: M&W Graphics, New York.

**Key:** B: Butterfields Auctioneers, 7601 Sunset Boulevard, Los Angeles; CI: Christie's Images, 1 Langley Lane, London; CLA: Christie's Los Angeles, 360 North Camden Drive, Beverley Hills; OPG: Octopus Publishing Group/Steve Tanner/Skinner Inc.; SC: Separate Cinema, Box 114 Hyde Park, New York; SK: Skinner Inc., Auctioneers & Appraisers of Antiques & Fine Art, Bolton, Massachusetts